Upholstery — a practical guide

Upholstery
— a practical guide

David & Freda Broan

Bishopsgate Press Ltd.
37 Union Street, London, SE1 1SE

ISBN 0 900873 48 5 (casebound)
0 900873 49 3 (limpbound)

All enquiries and requests relevant to this title should be sent to the publisher, Bishopsgate Press Ltd., 37 Union Street, London, SE1 1SE

Printed by Whitstable Litho Ltd., Millstrood Road, Whitstable, Kent.

Contents

Introduction

The aim of this book is to provide the beginner with a simple step-by-step guide to the techniques which underlie all upholstery work.

The series of projects provide a graduated course of practical experience which may later be applied successfully to larger items such as fireside chairs and settees.

Although at first sight upholstery may appear a complex undertaking, in fact, excellent results can be obtained by the amateur using a simple range of relatively inexpensive tools.

Stool

A small stool such as that shown in figure 1 offers a good introduction to basic upholstery techniques. It has a simple pad seat supported by webbing stretched across the wooden stool frame. Keep the old outer cover if this is available as it can be used as a pattern when cutting the new one at a later date.

Preparation

Using a ripping chisel and mallet, free the old cover by carefully lifting the tacks all around the stool frame. Next there should be a calico cover which is treated in the same way, followed by a layer of hair or flock wadding and a piece of hessian. This, when removed, will reveal the old webbing and the seat frame.

Carefully prise the old webbing loose and check the frame for loose joints or any other defects. All the old tacks should be removed where possible, though occasionally if, for example, the heads have come off, it may be preferable to leave the remains rather than risk damage to the wood.

Figure 2 shows the frame ready for work to begin.

1. Original condition of stool

2. Frame stripped down

1

2

Webbing

The function of the webbing is to support the padded seat above it. It bears most of the weight of the person sitting on the seat and should therefore be of the best quality available.

To fulfil its function properly the webbing needs to be adequately spaced, securely fixed and correctly tensioned.

As a general rule the gaps between the webs should be no greater than the width of the webbing itself. On this basis the stool will require two strips of webbing in each direction.

Using ⅝" improved tacks, take one end of a roll of webbing, turn back about 2", and tack to the side rail of the stool (figure 3). Five tacks should be used in a staggered pattern in order to minimize the likelihood of damage to the frame, (See figure 4). Do not cut the webbing from the roll at this stage.

Next, using the webbing stretcher, (see chapter on use of tools), stretch the webbing across the seat frame and tack with three tacks in a line to the opposite rail. (See figure 5). It should be tensioned enough to be tight, but without putting undue strain on the tacks holding it in place.

Release the stretcher and cut the webbing off the roll leaving again 2" to turn back. Fix with two tacks to once more complete the pattern shown in figure 4.

Following the same method add a second strip of webbing parallel to the first, and then two more at right angles, woven through to form the pattern shown in figure 6.

3.   Attaching the webbing

4.   Tacking pattern

5.   Stretching the webbing

6.   Webbing complete

10

Hessian

Cut a piece of 12oz. hessian about an inch and a half larger all round than the top of the stool and lay it in place over the webbing. Using fine half inch tacks, fix with a temporary tack in the centre of the back rail. Pull the hessian taut and put a temporary tack in the centre of the front rail. Deal similarly with the side rails and then the four corners. (Figure 7).

7. Hessian in place

When you are satisfied that the hessian is taut and square with the seat frame hammer the tacks home. Now turn in the spare material to form a hem along each edge of the frame and tack down, tucking in the corners neatly as you come to them. (See figure 8).

8. Turning in the hem

Bridle Ties

Whilst the hessian stops the stuffing from dropping down through the webbing, the bridle ties hold it in place from above and help the seat to keep its shape.

Thread a half-round or springing needle with a piece of No. 2 upholsterers twine long enough to go one and a half times around the seat frame. Start with a small stitch in one corner and tie a slip knot to secure the twine. Take the needle to the centre of an adjoining rail and make another small stitch to form the first tie. Work around the seat in this manner making a stitch at each corner and at the centre of each rail. (See figure 9).

9. Putting in bridle ties

Do not knot the twine and do not pull it tight. The loops should be just slack without being loose. When you reach the corner from which you started continue diagonally across the centre of the seat as shown in figure 10. Finally make a small stitch and tie the twine off securely.

10. Bridle ties complete

Stuffing

The traditional material used for stuffing upholstered furniture is horse hair. This compresses to form a firm, resilient, but springy mat, which makes an ideal basis for the seat. New horse hair or hair mixtures are expensive but an unwanted 'overstuffed' settee or armchair can often prove a fruitful source of supply. Re-used hair must be teased out carefully until it is of a light fluffy consistency before being incorporated in the work.

Taking small handfuls of hair at a time, tuck it under and around the bridle ties to form an even layer one and a half to two inches thick over the whole area of the seat. (See figure 11). Start by working around the edge of the seat frame, then in to the centre. The aim is to produce an even mat of hair without any lumps or thin places.

Tease the hair together with the fingers and press down gently with the flat of the hand to test for even thickness. Pay special attention to the edges and corners.

Calico

Now measure across the top of the stuffing and down to the polished edge of the wood on either side of the stool, add 4", (2" each side) and cut a square of calico to this measurement. Lay the calico over the top of the stool so that it hangs down evenly all round. Put a temporary ⅜" tack in the centre of one rail, then stretch the calico firmly over the seat and fasten similarly in the centre of the rail opposite. Do the same at the centre of the other two rails. Figure 12 shows the stool at this stage.

11. Picking in the stuffing

12. Putting on the calico cover

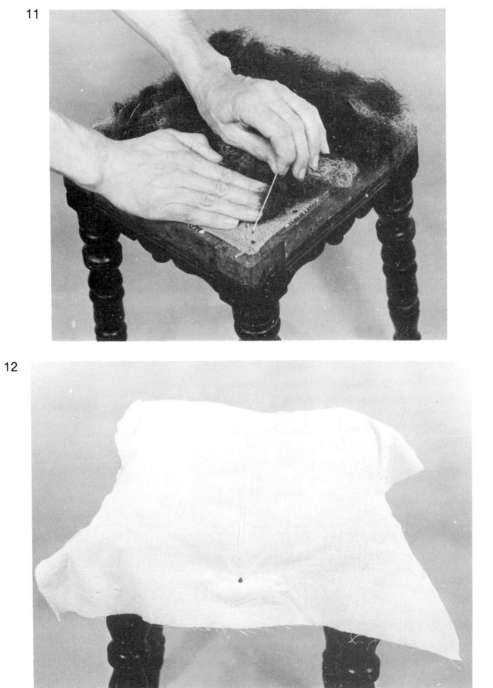

Taking each corner in turn, pull the calico down firmly and tack with a temporary tack as before, (See figure 13). Feeling through the calico from the top of the seat, check each corner to see that there is enough stuffing. You should not be able to feel the wood through. If there is not enough release the tack, add a little more hair and temporarily tack down again.

When you are satisfied with the corners, work along each rail in a similar manner, adding more hair where necessary or adjusting it with the regulator needle (figure 13). When all seems in order, put in temporary ⅜" tacks at one inch intervals along each rail pulling the calico tight as you go. Check that your tack-line is clear of the polished wood edge that you are working to and that the stuffing does not come down over the edge of the seatframe.

The aim is to get a smooth domed top to the stool with firm, well shaped edges and corners. Visualize the shape that the seat should have and then work towards it.

Neaten the corners by making little pleats in the calico where necessary, then hammer the tacks home and cut off the excess material all round, (figure 14). Finally cut a sheet of skin wadding to just fit the padded area of the seat and lay it on with the skin side uppermost. This stops any sharp ends of horse hair from working their way out through the cover. (Figure 15).

13. Adjusting the stuffing

14. Calico stage complete

15. Skin wadding in place

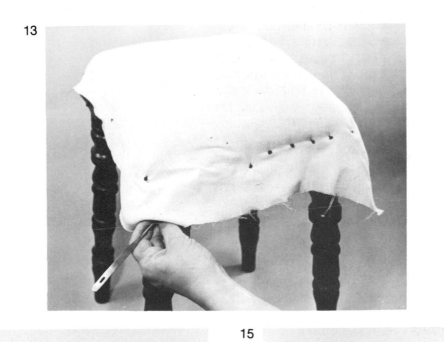

13

14

15

Final Cover

Cut a piece of cover material 2″ larger all round than the top of the seat and lay it in place. If there is a large pattern make sure that it is centrally placed. Put temporary ⅜″ tacks at the centre of each rail and at each corner pulling the material tight as with the calico cover.

16. Putting on the cover

When you are satisfied that the cover is square with the frame and evenly stretched, put in additional tacks along each rail close to the polished wood edge at one inch intervals, leaving the corners until last. Finish the corners by making two little pleats as shown in figure 16, the flat end of the regulator needle is useful here, then hammer the tacks home and cut off the excess fabric.

Cut a suitable piece of gimp or braid a little longer than will go all around the stool and carefully glue it in place to hide the heads of the tacks (figure 17). Start and finish in the centre of one rail and turn ½″ under at each end to prevent fraying. Two gimp pins will hold the ends secure and with care the heads can usually be arranged so that they are hidden in the weave of the gimp or braid.

17. Fitting the braid

Figure 18 shows the finished stool.

18. The finished stool

16

17

18

Drop-in Seat

This project is basically similar in the techniques used to the previous one but with one or two variations worthy of seperate consideration.

The seat is upholstered onto a wooden frame that is held in place by a peg set in the centre of the front rail of the chair. In the example shown in figure 19 the sides of the seat are bordered by the side rails of the chair whilst the front and back of the seat are open.

Preparation

Turn the seat upside down and carefully remove the old cover and lining. Now turn back, cut the bridle ties, and remove the stuffing, hessian and webbing. Check the joints of the frame and remove all tacks etc. If you have to reglue the frame make sure that it still fits into the chair when you have reassembled it before the glue dries. Figure 20 shows the cleared frame with peg-hole in front rail.

Webbing

Web the frame just as in the previous project starting with a centre strip (avoiding the peg hole) as shown in figure 21. Note that the outer strips from front to back are set at a slight angle to compensate for the increased width at the front of the frame. Do not forget to weave the side to side webbing through before you tack it on and turn the ends over so that they are square with the side of the frame.

19. Original condition

20. Seat frame

21. Webbing in place

19

20

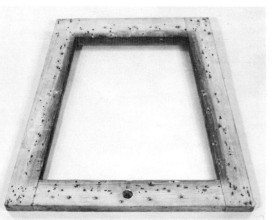

21

Hessian and Bridle Ties

Cut a square piece of 12oz Hessian 3″ wider than the front of the frame and 3″ deeper than the distance from front to back. Stretch it across the frame and tack at the centre of each rail and at each corner with temporary ½″ fine tacks. Make sure the weave is square with the front and back rails, turn back a hem all round, and tack down as shown in figure 22. Try the frame in the chair and if the peg needs to come through the hessian from underneath make a small cross shaped cut to allow it to do so.

22.   Hessian and bridle ties

Finally make bridle ties, just as for the stool, with No. 2 upholsterers twine. You will need a piece long enough to go one and a half times around the frame.

Stuffing

Taking small handfuls of horsehair, commence stuffing the seat, tucking the hair under and around the bridle ties. As the padding on the front rail will take most of the pressure this should be made very firm, whilst that on the side rails should be left a little softer so as to slope down the meet the chair frame.

23.   Stuffing in place

Aim for a smooth, even thickness of hair about two inches deep across the seat as a whole. Tease the hair together with the fingers and test for thin places by pressing down on the seat with the flat of the hand. It is well worth spending some time getting this stage just right as the ultimate success of the whole task depends upon it. Figure 23 shows the stuffing in place.

Calico

Cut a piece of calico large enough to cover the seat and leave a three inch margin all round. Lay it down flat and lay the seat upside down in the centre of it so that the front and back edges of the frame are square with the weave of the material.

Bring the front edge of the calico up and pin it in the centre of the front rail with a temporary ⅜″ tack. Then take the back edge of the calico and pulling it tight, pin it to the centre of the back rail in the same manner. Do similarly at the centre of the side rails and then at the four corners.

Turn the seat right way up and examine. The calico should now be stretched evenly and tightly over the frame. If not, release each tack as necessary and adjust. Check the stuffing for even thickness paying particular attention to the corners and rail edges. Add more hair if needed and adjust using the regulator needle as required. Aim for a good domed shape with gently sloping sides and a firm, evenly padded front rail.

Now stand the seat on its back edge and work along the front rail, pulling the calico tight with your right hand and shaping the edge of the padding with your left. As you work add more temporary tacks every 1½″ or so. (See figure 24). Deal similarly with the side rails and then the back.

Check that the stuffing does not come over the edge of the seat frame and that all is in order and then hammer the tacks home. Fold in the corners neatly, cutting away excess material as required. Make a little cross shaped cut in the calico where it covers the peg hole.

Finally cut a piece of skin wadding to fit the top of the seat and just come over the frame at the front and back. Lay this in place with the skin side uppermost.

24. *Putting on the calico cover*

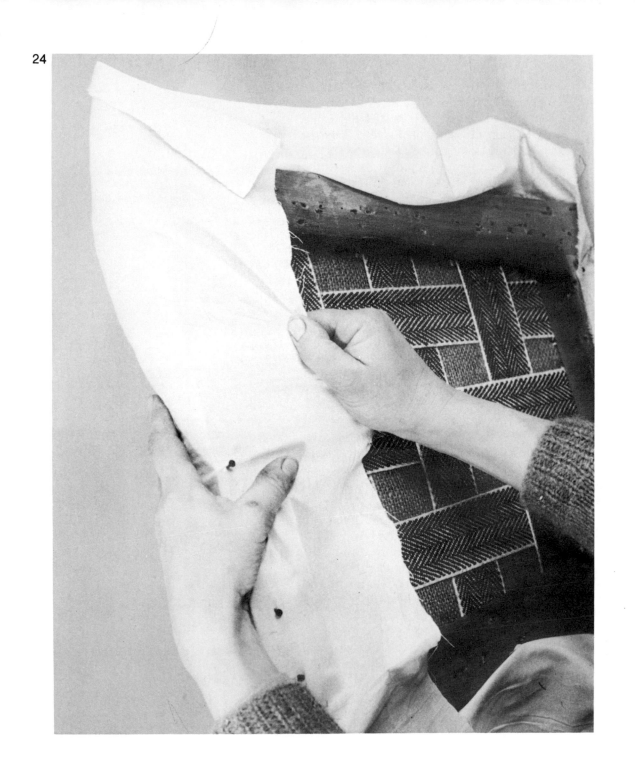

Cover

Cut a piece of cover material allowing a three inch margin all round making sure any pattern is centred. If there is a 'top' to the pattern it should come at the back of the seat. Lay the material upside down on a flat surface and lay the seat upside down on top of it. Attach the cover with temporary ⅜" tacks to the underside of the frame as for the calico. First at the centre of each rail, then at the corners, pulling the material tight as you go.

Turn over and check that pattern is square and centred then work around the frame tightening the cover and putting in temporary tacks every inch. Keep the tack line away from the frame edge and cut away excess material at the corners to make neat pleats as with the stool. When you are satisfied hammer the tacks home and cut away excess material all round. Make a small cross shaped cut for the peg.

Finishing

To neaten the underside of the seat cut a piece of black upholstery linen 1½" bigger all round than the bottom of the seat frame. Turning an inch under to form a hem at the front, tack with temporary ⅜" tacks along the front rail so as to hide the tacks holding the cover. Start with two tacks toward the centre about 1½" each side of the peg hole, then, pulling the fabric tight, two more tacks nearly out to the corners.

Turn excess material under at back to form hem and fix to back and side rails similarly. Hammer home the temporary tacks and add further tacks at 1¼" intervals to secure. Make a small slit at the front and turn material under to expose peg hole. Figure 25 shows this stage almost complete.

The finished chair is shown in figure 26.

25. *Lining back the underside*

26. *Completed seat*

26

25

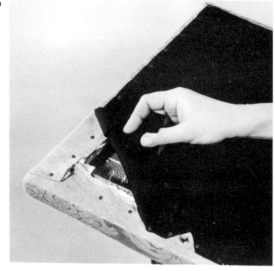

26

Side Chair

The chair shown in figure 27 introduces one of the most important basic upholstery techniques, the formation of a reinforced roll of padding around the edge of the seat frame. The method shown may also be applied to larger stools where additional support is needed.

27.   Original condition of seat

Preparation

The seat must be stripped down in the normal manner, the old coverings, stuffing and webbing being carefully removed. (Figure 28). Remove old tacks and check for loose joints. If the seat has been correctly upholstered in the past the outside top edge of each rail will be bevelled. If this is not so a bevelled edge $1/8''$ - $3/16''$ wide must be formed on each rail with a coarse file as shown in figure 29.

28.   Cleared frame

Webbing

Apply webbing to the top of the chair frame as with the drop-in seat. Begin with a piece from the centre of the back rail to the centre of the front. Then a piece each side of this spaced to allow for the wider front rail. Finally weave through the three pieces from side to side.

29.   Forming the bevelled edge

27

28

29

Hessian

Cut a piece of 12oz. Hessian 1½" larger all round than the seat frame. Turn forward a one inch hem at the back and tack with a temporary ½" tack to centre of back rail. Pull taut and tack at centre of front rail. Then similarly at centre of side rails. Now add more temporary tacks along each rail at about 2½" intervals keeping the hessian stretched tight. Leave the corners at present.

When you are satisfied the hessian is square and evenly stretched hammer home the tacks. Now turn in the excess material along the front and sides and tack down midway between the first set of tacks.

The front corners may be finished by turning back the hessian diagonally towards the centre of the seat as shown in figure 30 and then tacking down.

The back corners are turned in similarly but must be carefully fitted around the back uprights of the chair. (See figure 31).

Figure 32 shows this stage complete.

Forming the Edge Roll

The purpose of the edge roll is to reinforce the stuffing along the edges of the seat. This helps the seat to keep its shape and provides additional support over the hard wood edges of the rails.

30. *Hessian: Fitting the front corners*

31. *Hessian: Fitting the back corners*

32. *Hessian stage complete.*

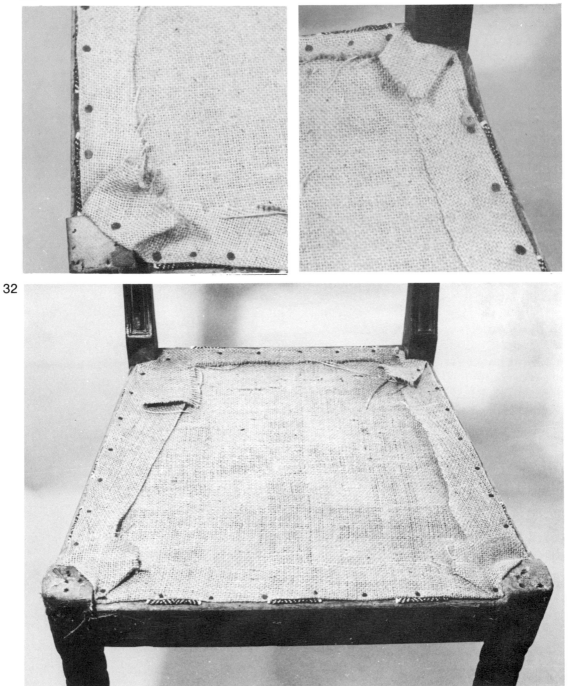

Scrim

Cut a piece of scrim 3″ wider all round than the top of the seat frame. Lay it in place so that it is central and the weave is square with the front and back rails. Fix with temporary tacks at the centre of each rail. (See figure 33).

With a felt tip pen and a straight edge mark on the scrim a border 3″ wide all the way around the seat. Take a half round needle and thread it with enough No. 2 twine to go around the chair frame. Start at one corner and sew the scrim to the hessian beneath it along the marked line of the border. Start with a small stitch and secure the end with a knot. Then use a simple running stitch about ½″ in length. (See figure 34). Be careful to avoid stitching through the webbing as you proceed. When you arrive back at the starting point tie the thread off.

Bridle Ties

You will now have a flap of scrim 6″ wide all the way round the frame. Turn this back in to the centre of the seat temporarily to expose the hessian border underneath.

Using a half round needle and No. 2 twine (enough to go one and a half times around the seat) make bridle ties around the border. Start with a small stitch at one corner and secure twine with a knot. Then take a stitch at the centre of an adjoining rail, then one at the next corner and so on, as with the stool (figure 9). Do not tighten the thread and do not knot except at beginning and end

33.   Scrim in place

34.   Sewing in progress

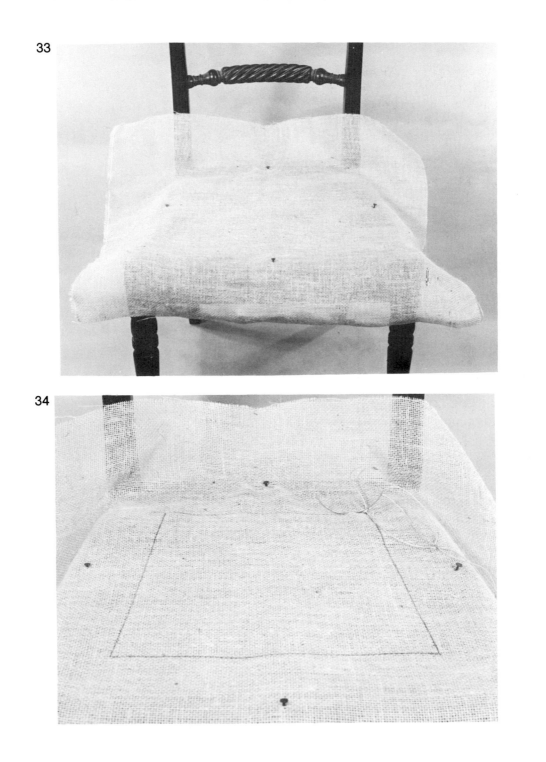

Stuffing

For stuffing the roll fibre is quite adequate and in the example shown algerian fibre was used.

Starting with the front rail take small handfuls of fibre, well teased out, and insert under and around the bridle ties. Build up a firm resilient pad of fibre paying particular attention to the edges and corners of the frame.

When the front rail is complete pull the scrim down tightly over it and fix with temporary tacks (See figure 35). Then deal similarly with the side rails and finish at the back.

35. Forming the edge roll

The roll should now be firm and even, about 3″ in diameter. Check for thin places, releasing the tacks and adding more fibre if needed. Use the regulator needle to adjust any unevenness or irregularities through the scrim.

Next, starting at the centre of the front rail, release the temporary tacks one or two at a time, turn the excess scrim under to form a hem and tack down onto the bevelled edge of the rail with ⅜″ tacks as shown in figure 36.

Continue along the side rails making sure the corners are well padded before finally tacking the scrim down over them. Lastly work from the centre of the back rail along to each corner. Here you will need to cut diagonally into each corner of the scrim just sufficiently to enable it to be pulled down snugly either side of the chair back.

36. Tacking back the scrim

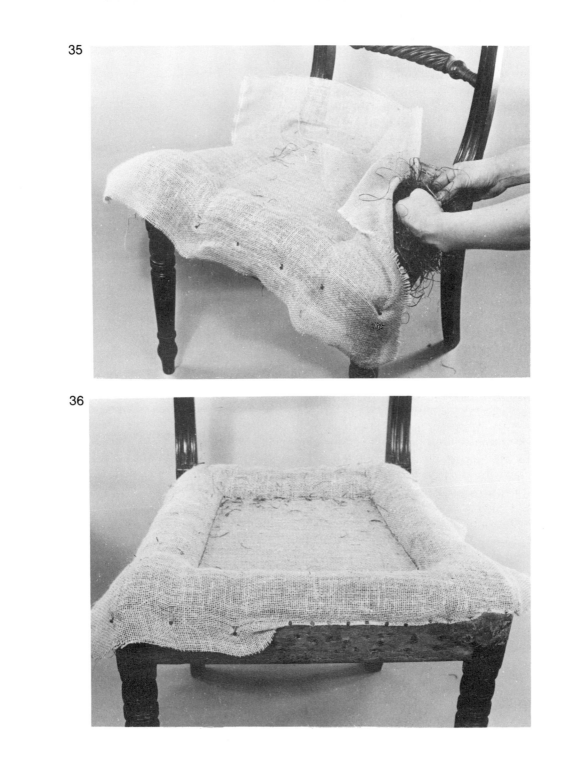

Stitching the Roll

To form the roll two kinds of stitching are used. First a 'blind' or 'sink' stitch which pulls forward and consolidates the fibre, and secondly a 'top' or 'roll' stitch which compresses the fibre and holds it in position on the edge of the rail.

37. Blind stitch 1

Blind Stitching

Thread a 10″ double bayonet needle with enough No. 2 twine to go one and a half times round the seat and start at the right hand end of the front rail about ½″ in from the corner.

Insert the needle about ¼″ above the rail and push it up diagonally through the roll towards the centre of the seat. When the point emerges through the top of the back of the roll pull it through until the eye of the needle is about three quarters of the way through the stuffing. Then move the eye to the right inside the roll and push the needle back down to emerge ¼″ to the right of its point of entry. Secure the end of the thread with a slip knot and pull tight. (See figure 37).

38. Blind stitch 2

Insert the needle 2″ to the left, still ¼″ above the rail. Push it diagonally up through the roll towards the back rail. (See figure 38).

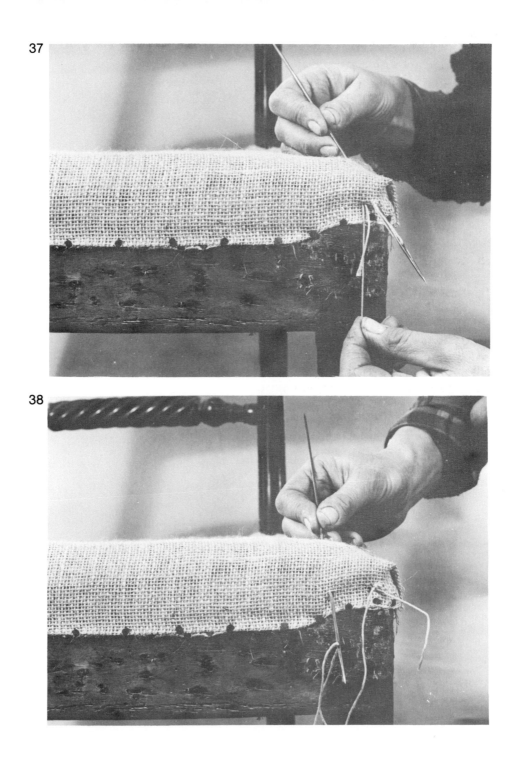

Pull through as before until the eye is three quarters of the way through the stuffing. Move eye to the right inside the roll and push needle back down to emerge midway between its point of entry and the original knot. Do not pull it right through but first take each end of twine from the stitch either side and wind each twice around the needle as shown in figure 39. Now withdraw the needle and tighten the knot so formed by pulling on the twine, first to the right and then to the left.

    Continue in this way making a line of blind stitches ¼″ above the front rail (figure 40). When you reach the left hand corner tie the twine off.

39. Blind stitch 3

40. Blind stitch 4

Top Stitching

To make the top stitch, work back along the front rail from left to right above the line of blind stitching.

    Using a similar length of twine insert the needle about ½″ from the left hand corner of the front rail a little above the line of blind stitching. Push the needle up and back through the roll until it emerges the other side (See figure 41). Pull it right through and then push it back down ¼″ to the left to emerge a similar distance from the original point of entry. Secure the end of the thread with a slip knot and pull tight.

41. Top stitch 1

Now insert the needle 2″ to the right and about ½″ above the line of blind stitching. Push it up and through the roll as before and when it emerges the far side pull it right through. Now reinsert the eye end of the needle an inch to the left and push it down through the roll to emerge midway between its point of entry and the original knot. Do not pull it right through but again wind the two ends of twine adjacent to it around the needle twice to form the knot. (See figure 42).

Now pull the needle through and tighten the twine first to the left and then to the right. Again insert the needle 2″ to the right and make further top stitches as described above.

You will need to use the regulator needle to adjust the amount of fibre picked up in each stitch so that the roll formed is of even thickness. It should be firmly compressed and about ¾″ to 1″ in diameter.

Figure 43 shows the top stitch in progress.

When you have completed the front rail work along the side and back rails in a similar manner, first blind stitch, then top stitch using the regulator needle to pull forward and adjust the fibre as required.

Secondary Stuffing

With the edge roll complete, the top of the seat is now padded in the normal way with horse hair.

42. Top stitch 2

43. Top stitch 3

Put in bridle ties around and across the area inside the edge roll as shown in figure 44. Taking small handfuls of well teased out horse hair insert them under and around the ties to form a firm resilient mat 1½" to 2" deep.

The aim is to get a good domed shape to the seat, sloping down smoothly from the centre to firm, evenly padded edges.

44. Secondary stuffing

Calico

Cut a piece of calico 6" larger all round than the top of the seat.

Lay it in place and fix with a temporary ⅜" tack in the centre of the underside of the back rail. Pull the calico tightly across the seat and secure under the centre of the front rail similarly. Do the same at the centre of the side rails, then add additional temporary tacks along each rail until the calico is evenly and tightly stretched across the seat.

Cut into each of the back corners of the calico diagonally to accommodate the uprights of the chair back, and turn the edges under, cutting away excess material as required.

45. Putting on the calico cover

At the front corners trim the material to fit neatly round each leg and make a small pleat to take up the fullness of the fabric on each rail.

Now check that the stuffing is smooth and even with no thin places. Release the tacks and add more hair if needed. Particularly watch the edges and corners.

When you are satisfied, add additional tacks along each rail at 1½" intervals and hammer home. Trim off excess material.

Finally cut a piece of skin wadding just large enough to cover the seat, trim to shape, and lay in place with the skin side uppermost.

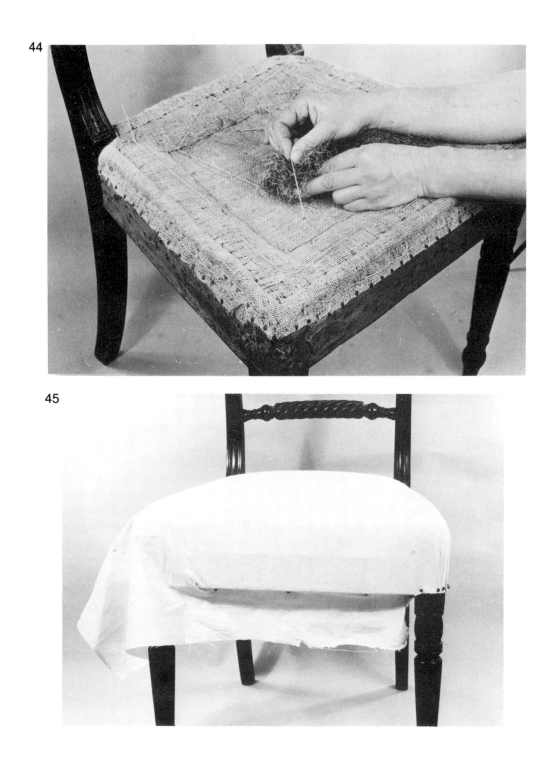

44

45

Cover

Cut a piece of cover material 6″ larger all round than the top of the chair. Take care that the pattern is centred and the right way up and that any pile brushes down towards the front of the seat.

Lay it in place and put in temporary ³⁄₈″ tacks under the rails as for the calico, pulling the material tight as you go.

Cut diagonally into the corners of the fabric to accommodate the chair back and, with the aid of the back of the regulator needle, turn the material under to fit snugly down around the frame. (See figure 46).

At the front corners, pull the material down over the frame and cut away excess to fit neatly to the top of the polished wood of the leg. Tack down with a ³⁄₈″ tack close to the edge of the material right on the corner. Make two small pleats to take up the fullness of the fabric on each rail so that they meet together at the corner. Tack closely around the top of the leg and trim off excess material. (See figure 47).

Add additional tacks under the rails at 1½″ intervals and hammer home. Trim off excess fabric.

Finishing

Glue a piece of braid around the bottom edge of the front and sides of the seat and a small piece along the back rail.

Turn the chair over and cut a piece of black upholstery linen 1½″ larger all round than the base of the frame. Use the same method of application as for the drop in seat but cut into each corner diagonally to allow a neat fit around the legs.

Figure 48 shows the chair completed.

46. *Fitting the cover 1*

47. *Fitting the cover 2*

48. *The finished chair*

46

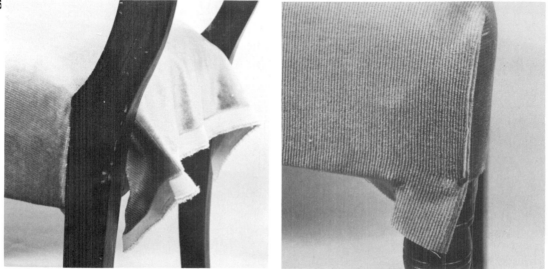

47

48

Arm Chair With Sprung Seat

The chair shown in figure 49 uses metal coil springs in addition to the normal padding to support the seat.

Preparation

Strip the chair back to the frame in the normal way and check for loose joints and split rails.

It is a good idea to make a note of the pattern of the springing for later reference as this may vary a little from chair to chair.

Check the springs for quality. If they are distorted or seem to have lost their resilience it is as well to replace them with new ones of the same size and gauge (wire thickness).

Make sure that the top of the frame has a bevelled edge to tack down onto at a later stage as with the side chair. If not, form one about ⅛″ — ³⁄₁₆″ wide using a coarse file (See figure 29).

Also note that the webbing on a sprung seat is fixed to the bottom of the rails to allow room for the springs within the body of the frame.

Figure 50 shows the cleared frame.

Webbing

On a sprung seat the spacing of the webbing is determined by the position of the springs. This is because each spring is set at the point where two strips of webbing cross one another.

Therefore the first step is to decide how the springs are to be placed in the seat. In this example six springs are used, three across the front of the frame, one in the centre and two to the rear. In a smaller seat the centre front spring may be omitted, but either way the aim is to provide even support across the whole seat area.

49. Original condition of seat

50. Cleared frame

46

49

50

Having decided on the springing pattern, turn the chair upside down and apply the webbing to the base in the same way as with previous examples.

Start with the centre piece, front to back, then the pieces either side of it. Lastly weave through and stretch the pieces from side to side. (Figure 51).

51. Webbing

Attaching the Springs

Take a springing needle and thread it with about two yards of No. 2 twine.

Stand the chair upright and facing you and set the springs in their positions on the crossing points of the webbing. The knots in the wire on top of the springs should be arranged to face in towards the centre of the seat.

Start at the back right hand corner and push the needle up through the webbing close to the base of the first spring. Make a small stitch over the wire of the spring and push the needle back down through the webbing to the underside. Fasten the end of the thread with a slip knot and pull tight.

Now move a quarter of the way round the spring to the next piece of webbing and stitch it to this in the same way. When you have finished the stitch, knot the twine to the long stitch that is formed underneath. Continue in this way around the spring until you have four equally spaced stitches as shown in figure 52.

52. Stitching in the springs

Take the twine across underneath the seat to the left hand back spring and stitch similarly. When this is complete move to the centre spring and then to the three front ones working from right to left. Secure each spring with four stitches and knot the twine to itself after each stitch. Tie the twine off when complete.

51

52

Lashing the Springs

In order to hold the springs steady and at the correct angle to one another they are now lashed to the frame with laid cord.

Knock three temporary 5/8" tacks into each rail, one in line with the centre of each spring or line of springs (See figure 53). Cut six pieces of laid cord each two foot longer than the width of the seat.

Take one piece of cord and tie the end tightly to the temporary tack at the front of the right hand rail with a double knot. Hammer the tack home.

Compress the right hand front spring slightly and knot the cord to it such that it leans a little towards the right hand rail. Now knot the cord to the opposite side of the spring, then to each side in turn of the centre spring, to each side of the left hand spring (compressing it slightly to match its opposite number), and lastly to the temporary tack at the front of the left hand rail. (See figure 53). Tie a double knot and hammer home.

Next lash the back two springs from side to side in a similar manner so that each leans slightly towards its side rail.

Put in the centre lashing from front to back, knotting the cord twice to each spring as you come to it and looping it round the previous lashings where they cross.

Now tie in the remaining two front to back lashings and lastly put in the centre lashing from side to side. Trim off the excess cord.

The seat should now have a domed shape with the centre spring upright and the others leaning slightly outward as shown in figure 54.

53. *Lashing the springs to the frame*

54. *Springs in place*

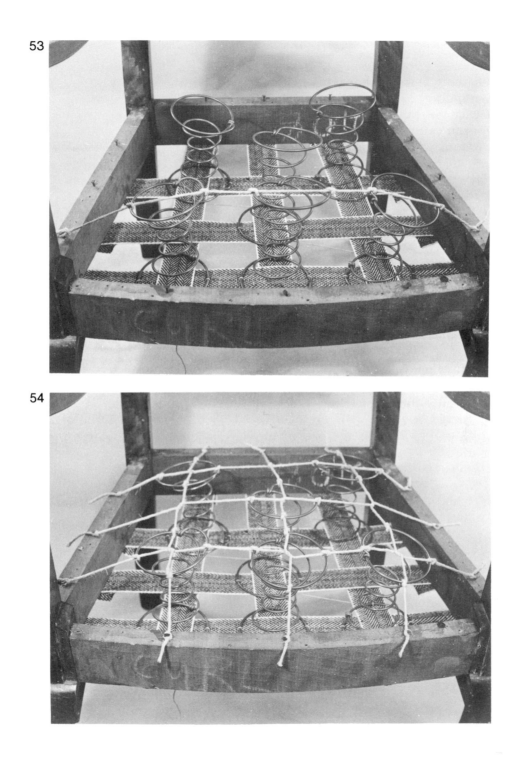

53

54

Hessian

Cut a piece of 12 oz. hessian 2″ larger all round than the seat frame. Lay it in place and fix with temporary ½″ tacks at two or three points on each rail, pulling the material tightly down over the springs.

When you are satisfied that it is tightly and evenly stretched, hammer the tacks home. Turn in the excess material to form a hem all round and tack down as shown in figure 55, folding in the corners neatly.

55. *Hessian*

Sewing in the Springs

The springs must now be sewn to the hessian in the same way as they were sewn to the webbing, except that three equally spaced stitches are sufficient for each spring.

Thread a half round needle with six foot of No. 2 twine and work from the back of the seat forwards as before.

Insert the needle through the hessian close to the spring, catch the spring in the stitch and bring the needle back through the hessian close on the other side. Tie the end of the thread with a slip knot and pull tight. Work three stitches round each spring in turn, knotting the twine as before after each stitch.

56. *Stitching the springs to the hessian*

Figure 56 shows the stitching in progress. Tie the twine off securely at the end.

Bridle Ties

With the springing installed the next step is to build up a good layer of padding across the top of the seat.

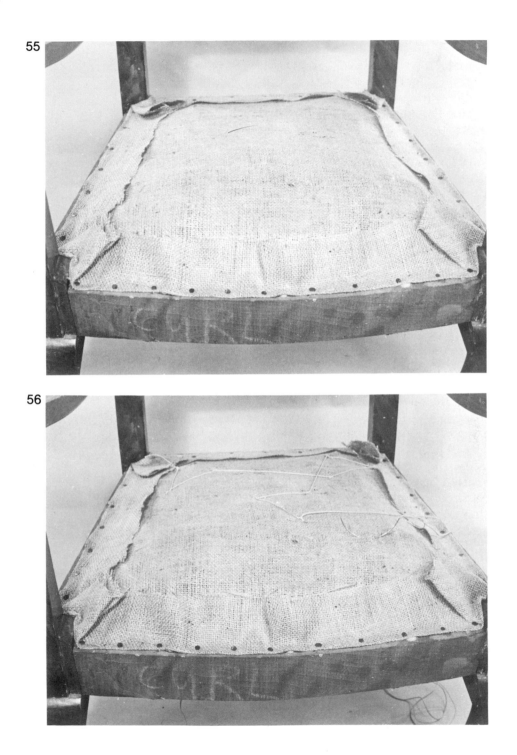

55

56

Thread a half round needle with enough No. 2 twine to go twice round the frame and sew in bridle ties. First work round the edge of the seat, then continue in a zig zag pattern across the central area. (See figure 57). Be careful not to pull the twine tight and knot only at the beginning and the end.

Stuffing

Fibre may be used for the stuffing and is built up around the bridle ties to form a thick mat 2″–2½″ deep all across the seat. Make sure there is a good depth of fibre round the edges and corners as they will need to be sewn at a later stage.

Figure 58 shows the stuffing nearly complete.

Scrim

Cut a piece of scrim 6″ larger all round than the top of the seat. Lay it in place and fix with a temporary tack at the centre of the back rail. Pull the scrim tightly forward over the stuffing and put a temporary tack in the centre of the front rail. Do similarly with the side rails.

Cut diagonally into each corner of the scrim, turn the excess under and fit neatly around each leg, pull tight and tack with temporary tacks (See figure 59).

Check carefully that there is a good even depth of fibre across the whole seat area, the edges and corners should be extra firm. Add more stuffing if required and adjust any unevenness through the scrim with the regulator needle.

Figure 59 indicates the full rounded appearance that should be achieved.

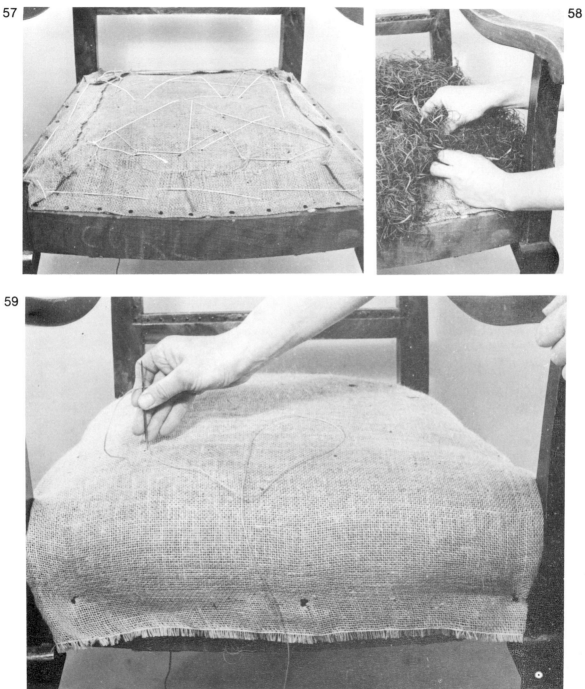

Stuffing Ties

These help to hold the fibre in place and con-solidate the centre of the seat.

Thread a double bayonet needle with 8ft of No. 2 twine and push it down through the seat about 5″ in diagonally from the front left hand corner of the frame (See figure 59).

Taking care to avoid the springs and the webbing, pull the needle just through the bot-tom hessian, then push it back up eye first through the seat about ¾″ to one side. Secure the end of the thread with a slip knot and pull tight.

Push the needle down through the seat again just to the left of centre of the front rail and in line with the first stitch. (About 4″ in from the front). Pull it through underneath as before and then push it back up, eye first, ¾″ to the right and pull tight.

Work around the frame in this manner tak-ing a stitch at each corner and at the centre of each rail, forming as it were, a border of stitch-ing about 4″ in from the edge of the seat.

Pull the twine tight as you go and be careful to avoid catching the springs or the webbing in the loops of twine underneath.

Finish off with a couple of stitches across the centre of the seat and tie the twine off securely. See figure 60.

Tacking Down the Scrim

Working along each rail in turn from front to back, remove the temporary tacks, turn under the excess scrim and tack down to the bevelled edge with ⅜″ tacks as in the side chair. Work from the centre of the rail out to each edge and pull the scrim down firmly as you work, adding more fibre if required to form a firm even roll of stuffing. Use the regulator needle to adjust any unevenness through the scrim. See figure 60.

60.   Stuffing ties

56

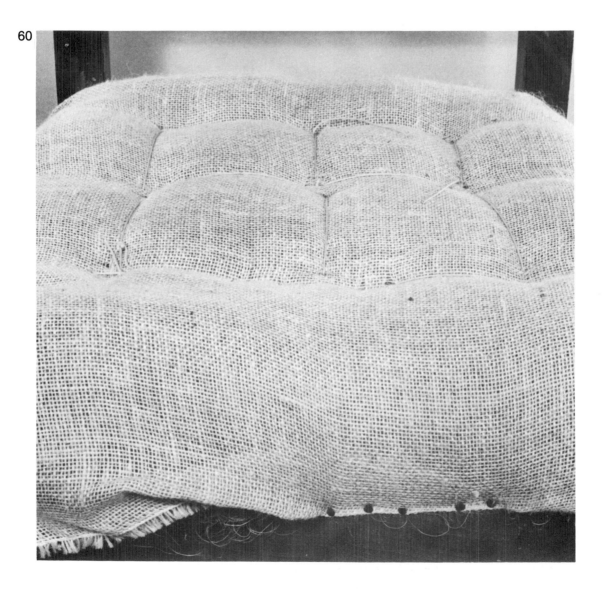

Stitching the Edge Roll

Thread a double bayonet needle with enough No. 2 twine to go one and a half times around the seat and starting at the right hand side of the front rail put in a row of blind stitching ¼" above the tack line in the same way as for the side chair.

Remember not to pull the needle right through the roll, make each new stitch 2" forward and each return stitch 1" back. Figure 61 shows this stage in progress with the twine looped around the needle to form the knot. Pull tight first to the right and then to the left. When the row is complete tie the thread off securely.

Now put in a row of top stitches, as for the side chair, to form the edge roll, pulling the stuffing forward as required with the regulator needle (See figure 62).

The roll formed should be firmly packed and of even height and thickness. Again make each new stitch 2" forward and each return stitch 1" back, but of course taking the needle right the way through the roll in between. Form the knot by winding the twine around the needle as before, tightening each stitch as you go.

Complete each rail in turn finishing at the back.

Bridle Ties and Stuffing

Thread a half round needle with enough No. 2 twine to go twice around the top of the seat and put in bridle ties over the area enclosed by the edge roll. Work first around the edge, then across the centre.

61. Blind stitching

62. Top stitching

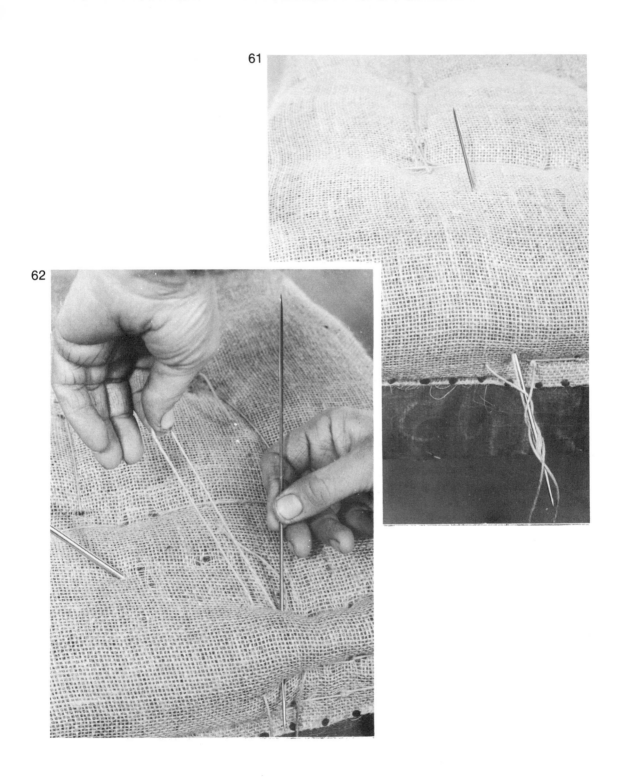

Put in small handfuls of hair under and around the ties, gradually building up a good layer of padding across the top of the seat to form a smooth, evenly domed shape. Along the edges and at the corners tease the hair together with the fingers, moulding it to the shape you want to fill out and meet the line of the edge roll.

Figure 63 shows this stage in progress.

Calico

Cut a piece of calico large enough to cover the seat and allow a margin all round. To determine the correct size first measure from the centre of the bottom edge of the front rail up over the seat and down to the same point on the back rail. Add 4″ to the measurement obtained.

Then measure from side to side across the seat in a similar manner at its widest point, just behind the front legs. Add 4″ to this measurement also.

Cut a piece of calico to this size and lay it in place on the seat. Fix it with a temporary ½″ fine tack under the centre of the back rail, then pull the calico tight and fix similarly under the centre of the front rail. Do the same at the centre of each side rail, then carefully cut diagonally into the material at each corner, pull tight and temporarily tack in place.

Check the stuffing for lumps or thin places, particularly around the edges and corners, add more hair if needed and adjust any unevenness with the regulator needle.

When you are satisfied add more tacks along the bottom of each rail at 1½″ intervals and hammer home.

Finally cut a piece of skin wadding to just fit over the seat area and lay it in place skin side uppermost. See figure 64.

63. *Secondary stuffing*

64. *Calico cover and skin wadding*

60

63

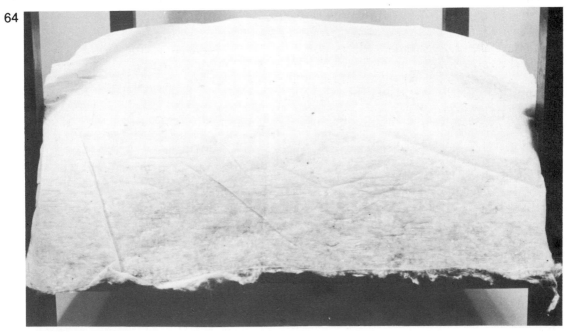

64

Cover

Cut a piece of cover material large enough to go over the seat and leave a 2″ margin all round. Work out the size that you need in the same way exactly as for the calico cover, bearing in mind that any pattern must come in the centre of the seat. If the fabric has a pile, it should lay towards the front rail.

Lay the cover in place and fix with temporary ⅜″ tacks under the centre of each rail, pulling the material tight as you go. Carefully cut in the front corners, trimming and turning under the edges to fit snugly down beside each leg and fix with temporary tacks under the front and side rails.

Do similarly with the back corners, smoothing the fabric back and out until it is evenly stretched across the seat.

At each stage check that the fabric is still square with the seat and the pattern central.

Finally add more tacks at 1½″ intervals along each rail and hammer home.

65. Finished seat

Finishing Off

Turn the chair over and finish the base in black upholstery linen as with previous examples.

Figure 65 shows the completed chair.

Prie Dieu

The prie-dieu or kneeler shown in figure 66 consists, from the upholsterers' point of view, of a strongly webbed and padded platform at the base and a smaller, shaped, firmly padded area on the top rail.

The kneeling area must be capable of supporting considerable localised pressure whilst the padded top rail must retain its shape adequately in use.

Preparation

Carefully remove the old cover and set aside for reference, then strip down to the frame as shown in figure 67. Make sure that there is a bevelled edge 1/8" wide along the top edge of each rail and around the padded area above. Check for loose joints and any damage to the frame.

Kneeling Area

The techniques used in this part of the work are basically similar to those used in the side chair. Therefore the stages are only outlined below to avoid undue repetition. For more detailed instructions at a particular stage see the relevant section of chapter 3.

Webbing and Hessian

Apply webbing to the frame using 5/8" improved tacks. First the pieces from front to back starting in the centre and working outward, then those woven through from side to side. If possible space the webbing a little more closely than usual to provide extra support.

66. Original condition

67. Cleared frame

66

67

Cut a piece of 14oz. hessian 1½" larger all round than the top of the frame and fix with temporary ½" fine tacks at the centre and towards the ends of each rail, stretching the hessian tightly across the frame. When it is evenly stretched hammer the tacks home. Turn in the excess material to form a hem and tack down, fitting the corners neatly round the uprights at the back as shown in figure 68.

68. *Hessian and webbing in place*

Forming the Edge Roll

Cut a piece of scrim 3" wider all round than the top of the frame and fix in place with 4 temporary tacks. Draw in a border on the scrim 3" wide all around the frame with a felt tip pen and sew the scrim to the hessian as before.

Turn back the scrim border, put in bridle ties around the edge of the hessian underneath and pad firmly and evenly with fibre. As you proceed pull the scrim down over the stuffing and fix with temporary tacks. Check for thin places and adjust as necessary. The roll should be firm and quite full at this stage.

When you are satisfied, work along each rail turning the scrim in, pulling it tight, and tacking it down along the bevelled edge with ⅜" tacks.

69. *Forming the edge roll*

Make a row of blind stitches along each rail about ¼" above the tack line and following the contours of the rail. Above this put in a row of top stitches, pulling the fibre forward with the regulator needle as required.

Figure 69 shows the work in progress.

Secondary Stuffing and Calico

Put in bridle ties around and across the area enclosed by the edge roll and pad thickly and firmly with horse hair. Remember that most of the pressure will come in the centre of the kneeler and therefore this area will need extra support.

66

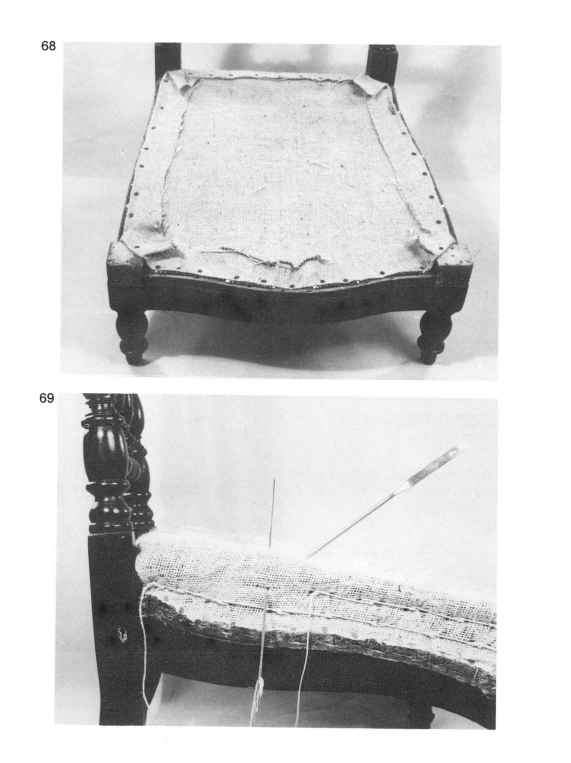

Cut a piece of calico 3″ wider all round than the top of the frame and fasten at the centre of each rail with temporary ⅜″ tacks, stretching the fabric tightly over the stuffing as you go. Add more tacks towards the ends of each rail, carefully cutting in the back corners and making neat pleats at the front as for the stool.

Check that the stuffing is firm and even, adding hair or adjusting with the regulator needle. The edges and corners should be smoothly and evenly padded and a good shape

When all is in order tack down to about ½″ above the polished wood edge. (See figure 70).

Cut a piece of skin wadding to fit and lay it in place skin side uppermost.

70. Calico cover

Cover

Cut a piece of cover material 3″ larger all round than the top of the kneeler and lay it in place. Check that the pattern, if any, is central, and that the pile lays from the back toward the front.

Stretch the cover over the frame fixing with temporary tacks at rail centres and then working out toward the corners. Fit the material around the front corners with small pleats to take up the fullness as with the stool. At the back cut diagonally into the material, turn under the excess, and fit snugly against the uprights.

When the cover is firmly and evenly stretched in place tack down close to the polished wood edge with ⅜″ tacks. Pin and glue gimp or braid to cover the tack line and finish the base in black upholstery linen.

Figure 71 shows this stage complete.

71. Kneeling area complete

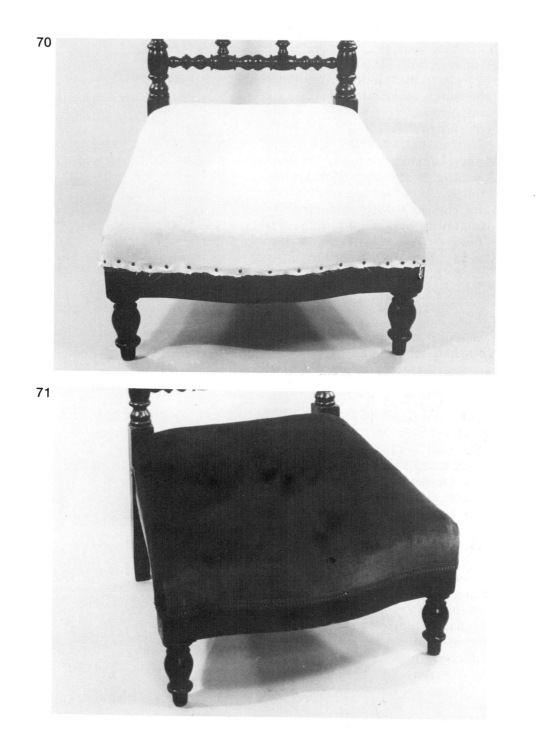

70

71

Padded Top Rail

The method used for this part of the work may also be applied to the padded areas that are sometimes found on the arms of chairs.

Bridle Ties and Stuffing

Put in bridle ties across the top of the area to be padded using short pieces of No. 2 twine as shown in figure 72.

Start by inserting ⅝" temporary tacks where the ends of each tie are to come. Then tie short pieces of twine between each pair of tacks leaving enough slack that the centre of the tie can be lifted about an inch from the wood. Hammer the tacks home.

Take small handfuls of fibre, well teased out, and insert them under and around the bridle ties in the usual manner, building up a good, thick layer of padding about 2" deep. Pay particular attention to the edges and rounded ends of the rail.

72. Bridle ties and stuffing

Scrim

Cut a piece of scrim 3" wider all round than the padded area and secure in place with temporary tacks, pulling it firmly down over the fibre stuffing. Care should be taken to accommodate the curved shape of the rail without distorting the weave of the scrim. (See figure 73).

Check for thin places in the stuffing adjusting with the regulator needle where necessary. A firm, rounded, symmetrical shape is needed with good coverage at the edges.

When you are satisfied, start at the centre of the rail, release the tacks, turn the excess scrim under, and tack down to the bevelled edge with ⅜" tacks. At the ends make tiny pleats to take up the fullness of the scrim on the curve.

73. Scrim in place

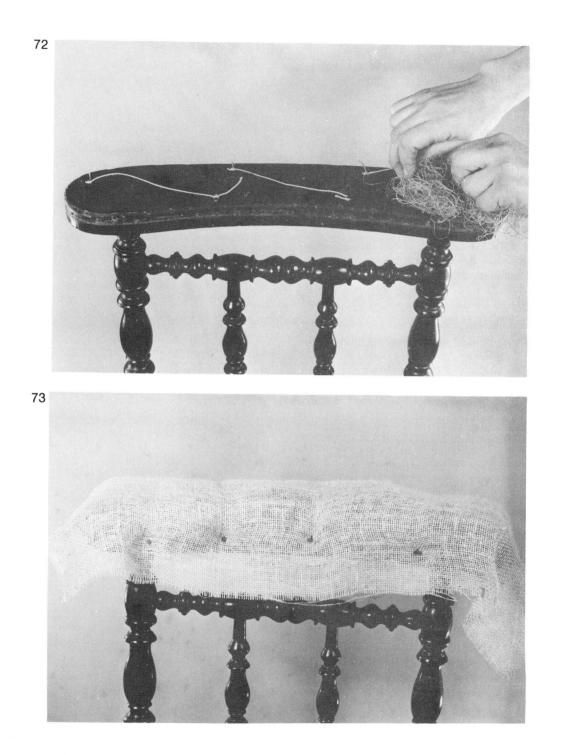

Stitching and Horse Hair

To help the padding to keep its shape sew in a
row of top stitches all round in the same way as
when making the edge roll for the kneeling
platform. Work to produce a good, even,
symmetrical outline, adjusting the fibre with
the regulator needle as you go.

74. *Top stitches and horse hair*

When complete, pad out the top of the sewn
area with horse hair to produce a smooth,
even, finish. See figure 74.

Calico

Fit a calico cover in the usual way, as with the
stool for example, adjusting the top layer of
hair until a good shape is obtained. Make a
series of small pleats at each end of the rail to
take up the fullness of the fabric and tack
down a little above the polished wood edge
with ⅜" tacks.

75. *Prie Dieu complete*

Cut a piece of skin wadding to shape to just
cover the padded area and lay in place skin
side uppermost.

Cover

Cut a piece of cover material 3" larger all
round than the top of the padding and lay it in
place. Fit it carefully to the rail with temporary ⅜" tacks, stretching it firmly and evenly
into place and taking care not to distort the
weave of the fabric in accommodating the
curve of the rail. Tack down just above the
polished wood edge, pleating the ends neatly
as with the calico.

Glue a piece of gimp or braid in place to
cover the tack line, starting and finishing in
the centre of the rail.

Figure 75 shows the prie dieu complete.

74

75

Box with Padded Lid

The box shown in figure 76 can be considered in two sections. The lid, consisting of a simple wooden frame which is webbed and then padded and buttoned and the box itself which is to be covered in matching fabric.

The Lid

The first thing to decide is the number and arrangement of buttons to be used. The buttons will need to be obtained from an upholsterers' suppliers who will also cover them for you.

If you have not got an original cover to work from it is as well to draw out a simple plan such as that shown in figure 77.

The arrangement has 4 rows of 2 buttons each 9″ apart, with 3 single buttons set midway between each pair.

Whatever pattern you choose the buttons should be equally spaced and evenly distributed over the padded area leaving a reasonable margin all round.

Webbing and Hessian

Web the top of the lid frame in the usual way using ⅝″ improved tacks but arrange the strips of webbing such that they coincide with the lines of the buttoning. This means that each button can be sewn through the webbing which gives it a strong anchorage.

The simplest way to do this is to first mark in the buttoning lines on the top of the lid frame (ie. the dotted lines shown in figure 77). The webbing can then be matched up to these as you proceed.

76. Original Condition

77. Plan of buttoning

76

77

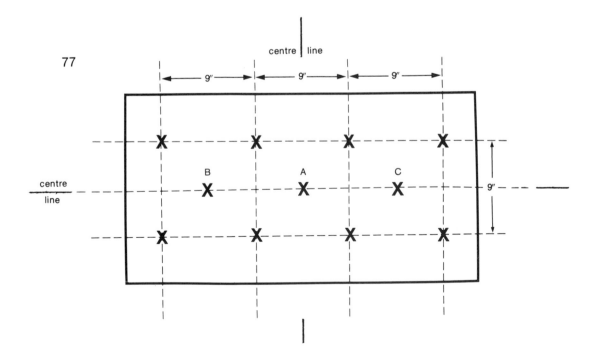

centre line

9″   9″   9″

B   A   C

centre
line

9″

First stretch and tack the short pieces from front to back. Start with a piece between each pair of buttoning marks then add more strips as required.

Next weave through, stretch and tack the long pieces from side to side, again working to the buttoning marks.

Cut a piece of hessian 1½" larger all round than the top of the frame and lay it in place. Stretch it evenly across the lid and tack down with ½" tacks, turning in a hem all round. See figure 78.

78. *Webbing and hessian in place*

Stuffing and Scrim

Using a half round needle, put in bridle ties across the whole top area of the lid. Make the ties about 6" long and work first around the edge of the frame, then in a random, zig-zag pattern across the centre. You will need enough No. 2 twine to go about two and a half times around the lid for this. Do not pull the ties tight and secure only at beginning and end.

Take small handfuls of horse hair, well teased out, and pick it in, under and around the ties, over the whole area. Build up a good thick layer of hair at least 2"–3" deep, bringing it well out to the edges and corners.

79. *Tacking down the scrim*

Cut a piece of scrim 3" wider all round than the top of the lid and fix in place with temporary tacks, pulling it down firmly over the stuffing. Make sure there is sufficient hair on the edges to give a good, full, rounded shape and that there are no thin places. Add more hair where required and adjust any unevenness with the regulator needle.

Now free the tacks a few at a time, turn under the excess scrim and tack down to the bevelled edge with ⅜" tacks. Work from the centre of each rail out to the corners as shown in figure 79.

78

79

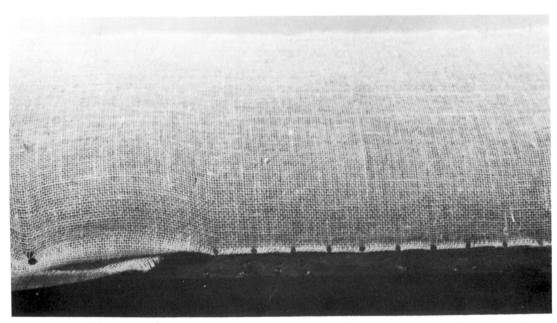

Stitching the Edge Roll

Put in a row of blind stitching along each side of the lid, just above the tack line as described in chapters 3 and 4

Then add a row of top stitches to form a firm, even edge to the padding. Use the regulator needle to adjust the stuffing as you go to produce a roll of even height and thickness. See figure 80.

80. Stitching the edge roll

Buttoning

There are two forms of buttoning commonly met with in this type of work.

Star or Float buttoning, where the buttons are applied to the surface of the padding after the cover is in place.

Deep buttoning, where the buttons are pulled down into the padding as the cover is put on, thus forming the characteristic diamond pleating between the buttons.

Star or float buttoning is much the simplest for a first attempt and has therefore been used for the box lid. However, the method used in deep buttoning is described in chapter 7 and may easily be substituted at this point if you wish. It is not easy to obtain good results on a large surface without some practice.

81. Wadding in place

Wadding and Calico

Cover the top of the lid with a thick layer of soft cotton wadding. Alternatively use a sheet of polyester wadding cut to size and fitted in place to make a smooth even surface to the top of the box. See figure 81.

Cut a piece of calico 3″ larger all round than the top of the lid, stretch it in place and tack down to the edges of the lid frame.

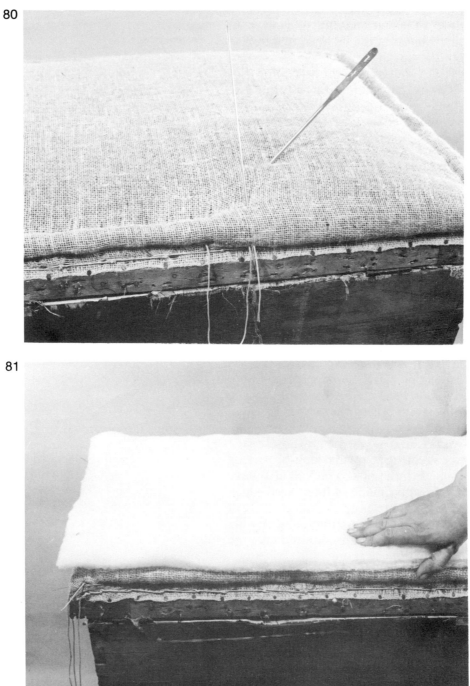

Cover

Cut a piece of cover material 6″ wider all round than the top of the lid and lay it upside down on a flat surface.

Referring to your plan of the buttoning (See figure 77) draw in the centre lines from top to bottom and from side to side with tailors' chalk on the back of the cover. Where the two lines cross is the position of the centre button A. Measure 9″ either way of this and mark in the positions B and C.

Now draw in a line 4½″ above the centre line from side to side and another 4½″ below it. This gives you the other two buttoning lines.

Next draw in lines from top to bottom 4½″ either side of the centre line and then 13½″ (4½+9) either side of the centre line.

This will give the position of all the buttons as shown on the plan.

Using a slipping needle put in tailors' tacks to mark the position of each button through the cover. All that is necessary is to make two small stitches one along each guideline of the plan, so that they cross on the front of the fabric at the point where the button is to go. See figure 82.

Remove the lid from the box by unscrewing the screws securing it to the hinges, leaving these attached to the box. You will also have to remove the stays made of linen tape which support the lid when it is open. Make a note of their present fixing position on the lid and the box and if they are old or discoloured take the opportunity to replace them.

Lay the cover in place on the lid making sure that it is square and centred. The best way is to mark in the centre point of each side of the lid on the wood of the frame and then match up the centre lines marked on the back of the cover to them.

82.   Putting in tailors' tacks

83.   Fitting the cover

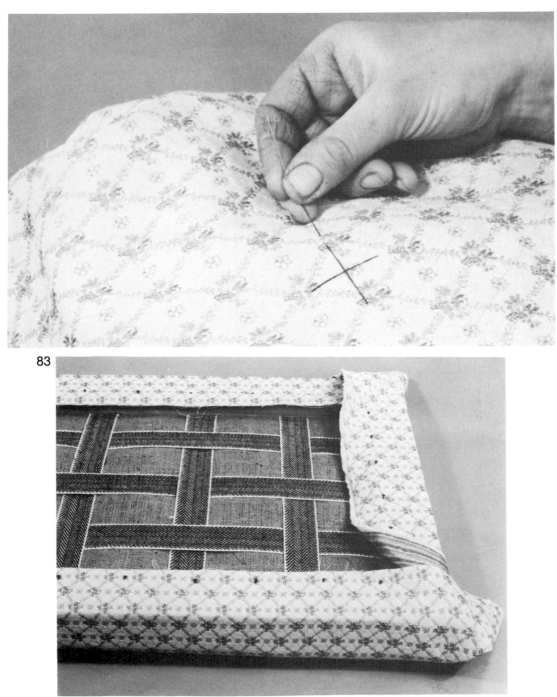

82

83

Stretch the cover over the frame and fix with temporary tacks underneath each rail. When you are satisfied that it is square, centred and evenly stretched, check for thin places or unevenness in the wadding and then tack down with ⅜" tacks close to the inside edge of the rail underneath the lid. See figure 83.

84.   Finishing the corners 1

At the corners proceed as follows: Take the corner of the cover, pull tight over the corner of the lid and tack down close to the inside edge of the frame. Take up the fullness of the material on one side of the corner with a pleat, cutting away excess material as necessary underneath and tack down well away from the edge of the frame. Figure 84.

85.   Finishing the corners 2

Do the same with the other side of the corner, tucking the material back underneath itself as shown in figure 85.

Sewing in the buttons

Cut a 15" length of fine twine and thread a button onto it so that the ends are of equal length. Thread both ends of the twine through the eye of a straight buttoning needle (a double bayonet needle will do), and push the needle right down through the lid at the point A on your plan (See figure 77). If you have got the webbing stage right it should emerge through the centre strip underneath. Remove the tailors' tacks, then tie the ends of the button twine together with a slip knot and pull tight, inserting a small, folded, piece of hessian (called a 'tuft') between the threads under the knot. This stops the knot pulling back through the webbing. See figure 86.

86.   Buttoning

Put in all the buttons in a similar manner working from the centre outwards and trim off the excess twine underneath except for the centre buttons A, B and C.

84

85

86

Lining

The lid should now be lined back to conceal the underside of the upholstery. Usually a plain fine-grained fabric is used that will harmonize with the colour of the cover. To add interest and help support the large area of fabric involved, two or three buttons, covered in the same fabric, can be used to pin the lining back to the inside of the lid.

Cut a piece of fabric about an inch and a half larger all round than the size of the lid so that you have enough to turn a hem under. Stretch it across the frame and fix with four $\frac{3}{8}''$ temporary tacks, one at the centre of each rail.

When you are satisfied that it is square, take the eye end of the double bayonet needle and push it down through the centre of the lining directly over the back of button A. Feel under the fabric from one corner for the ends of twine you have left to ascertain the right place.

Now release the temporary tack at one side, turn the fabric back, thread the twine ends through the eye of the needle and draw them through the lining to the outside. See figure 87.

Restretch the lining and find the correct position for the second button at B, insert the needle and bring the ends of twine through in a similar manner.

When all three sets of threads have been brought through the lining may be tacked down in the usual way, turning under a neat hem at the edge as you go. As you work along the ends of the lid, refit the linen stays, so that the tacks attaching them are just concealed under the edge of the lining. See figure 88.

Thread each button onto one of each pair of threads, make a knot and pull tight so that the fabric is held back in place. Do button A first, then B and C, trim the excess thread closely under each button.

87. Lining back the lid

88. Refitting the stay to the lid

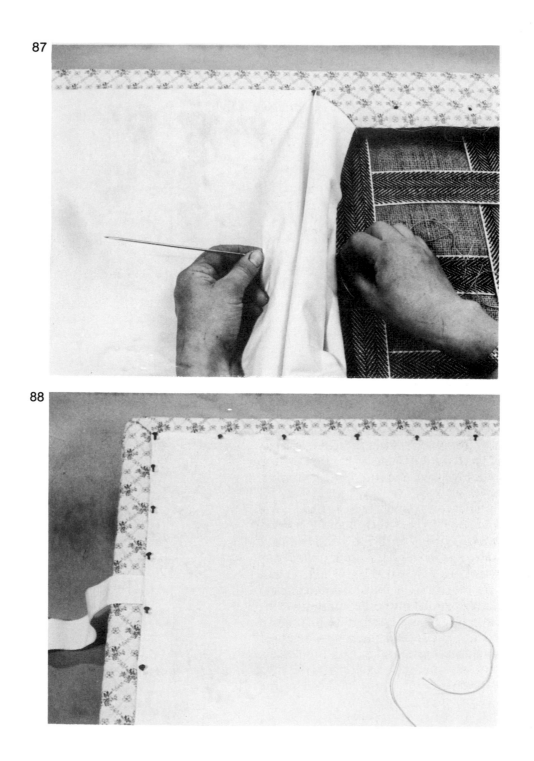

Glue braid or gimp around the edge of the lining to conceal the tack line and refit the lid to its hinges, using the point of the regulator needle to part the fibres of the cover fabric over the screw holes.

Covering the Box

89. *Back tacking*

Remove the lid from the box, this time leaving the hinges attached to the lid. Also unscrew and remove the feet.

Cut a piece of cover material 2″ wider all round than the front face of the box making sure that the pattern is the right way up, and square with the top edge of the material.

The method used to attach the panel to the top edge of the box is called back-tacking and results in the tacks used being hidden by the material itself.

Turn the panel upside down and lay it inside the box with the top edge of the material toward you such that it lays along the top edge of the box front. Put in 3 or 4 temporary tacks· to hold it in place. (See figure 89).

Cut a length of back-tacking strip to exactly fit along the front top edge of the box (a strip of stiff card will do) and mitre the corners. Tack it in place using ⅜″ tacks spaced at 1½″ intervals such that the top edge of the cover panel is sandwiched between it and the wood, (See figure 89). Be careful to keep the back edge of the strip level with the back edge of the box top.

90. *Fitting the front panel*

Turn the box onto its back, bring the front cover panel forward into place thus covering the back-tacking strip, pull it tightly down over the front and tack to the base of the box. Turn the margins of fabric at each side of the panel over onto the ends of the box and tack down similarly. Trim off excess fabric at the corners as necessary (See figure 90).

89

90

Now cut and fit the back panel in the same way but leave a small gap in the back tacking strip where each hinge fastens to the edge of the box.

Cut the end panels, allowing a 2″ margin. all round and fit to the box along their top edges similarly but cut the back-tacking strip off square ½″ short at each end. Pull each panel down over the box end and tack along the base leaving the last 3″ at each side free for the present.

Turn the margin of fabric at each side of the panel under to form a hem in line with the corner of the box, pulling the fabric tight and pinning it in place as you go. (See figure 91). Cut away excess material at the top and bottom, folding the edge of the fabric under to form a neat mitre at the corner on the top edge of the box.

With a slipping needle and thread to match the colour of the cover sew the panels together down each corner of the box. Work from the top downwards making tiny stitches as shown in figure 92. Note that the stitches themselves are always hidden by the fabric of one panel or the other.

When you have completed the slipping tack down the remaining sections of the end panels along the base of the box. Turn the box upside down, cover the botton with black upholstery linen and replace the feet. Refit the lid and reattach the linen stays to the box.

Figure 93 shows the work complete.

91. *Fitting end panel showing pinned edges.*

92. *Slip stitching*

93. *Box complete*

91

92

93

Deep Buttoned Stool

The small stool shown in figure 94 makes a good subject upon which to practise the technique of deep buttoning.

94.   *Cleared stool frame*

The early stages of the upholstery are identical to those described in detail in the previous chapter for the lid of the box.

First draw up a simple plan of the buttoning as shown in figure 95.

Next mark the position of the main buttoning lines (dotted on the plan) onto the frame of the stool and arrange the webbing to coincide with these.

Over the webbing stretch a piece of hessian, put in bridle ties and pick in a thick layer of horse hair over the seat area.

Cut a piece of scrim 3″ larger all round than the top of the stool, stretch it over the stuffing, turn under the excess and tack down to the bevelled edge of the frame.

95.   *Plan of buttoning*

Sew in a row of blind stitches just above each rail and then a row of top stitches to make a good firm edge.

Refering to your plan, carefully measure and mark in with a felt tip pen the position of the buttons on the top of the scrim. At each point cut a small hole in the scrim with a pair of sharp, pointed scissors. See figure 96.

Cover the top of the stool with a good layer of soft cotton wadding and break through small holes with the fingers where the buttons are to come. Alternatively a sheet of polyester wadding may be cut to size to just fit the top of the seat and holes made in a similar manner.

96.   *Preparing the scrim for buttoning*

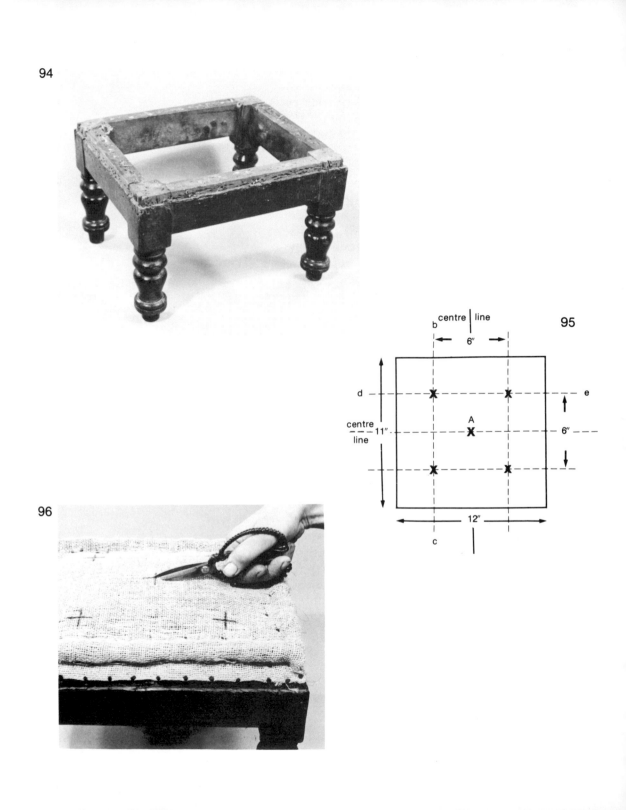

94

95

b centre line

6"

d ────── ✖ ✖ ────── e

A
centre ──11"── ✖
line

c

12"

6"

96

Preparing the Cover

Prepare a piece of cover material as follows: First work out the size required bearing in mind that an allowance must be made for the material taken up by the depth of the buttoning. How much to allow depends both upon the amount of give in the fabric and the depth of buttoning employed. Anything between 1½"–3" per button may be required. In this example a 2" allowance per button was made.

Refering to the plan (figure 95), the distance from front to back of the stool (11") is represented by the buttoning line b-c. There are two buttons to allow for, thus the front to back measurement of the cover will be : 11" + 4" (2 × 2" allowance) + 6" (3" margin each side) = 21".

The side to side measurement, represented by line d-c will be: 12" + 4" (2 × 2" allowance) + 6" (3" margin each side) = 22"

Note that the allowance for button A takes care of itself as the button is placed between the main buttoning lines.

Cut a piece of cover material 21" × 22" and lay it upside down on a flat surface. With tailors' chalk mark in the centre lines from top to bottom and side to side on the back of the cover. This will establish the position of button A. See figure 97.

On the plan (figure 95), the buttons are 6" apart. Take half this measurement plus half the buttoning allowance (3" + 1" = 4") and draw a line from top to bottom of the material either side of the centre line at this distance.

Do the same from side to side. The crossing points of the four lines give the positions of the remaining buttons.

Put in tailors' tacks at each button mark as in the previous chapter.

97. *Marking out the cover*

98. *Buttoning*

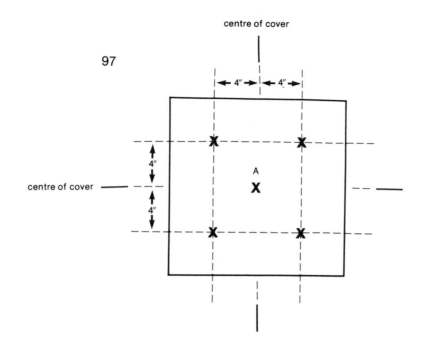

97

centre of cover

4″ ← → 4″

4″

4″

centre of cover

A
X

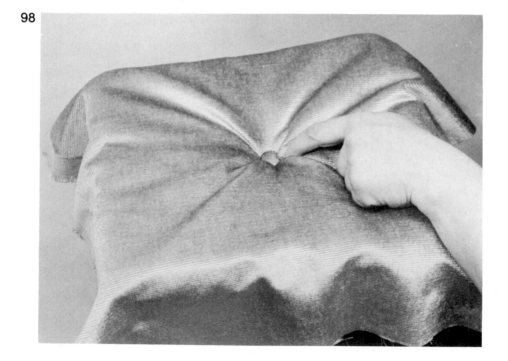

98

Buttoning

Lay the cover in place on the stool and thread a button onto a 20" length of fine twine. Thread both ends of the twine through the eye of a buttoning or double bayonet needle and insert it down through the centre buttoning mark A on the cover. Push it through the appropriate hole in the wadding and down through the seat to emerge through the webbing underneath.

Remove the tailors' tacks and pull the twine tight, gently easing the button and cover down into the padding of the seat. See figure 98. For the time being tie the twine to a temporary tack in the stool frame.

Take the next button and insert in the same way, folding the fullness of the material away into a pleat between the two buttons. See figure 99. Use the back of the regulator needle to help fold the material into place.

When all the buttons and centre pleats are in place, work around the edge of the stool folding in edge pleats to take up the fullness of the fabric against each button (See figure 100). Bring the pleat out at right angles to the rail of the seat and pin in place.

Check that all the buttons are the same depth and adjust if necessary by tightening any that are too shallow. Then tie off each set of twines at the back as with the box lid, inserting tufts of folded hessian under each knot to prevent it pulling back through the webbing.

Stretch the edges of the cover into place and tack down with ³⁄₈" tacks close above the polished wood edge, cutting in the corners and making neat pleats as with the stool. Trim off excess material and glue braid or gimp in place to cover the tack line.

Finish the underside with black upholstery linen. Figure 101 shows the stool complete.

99. Forming the pleats

100. Making the edge pleats

101. Finished stool

94

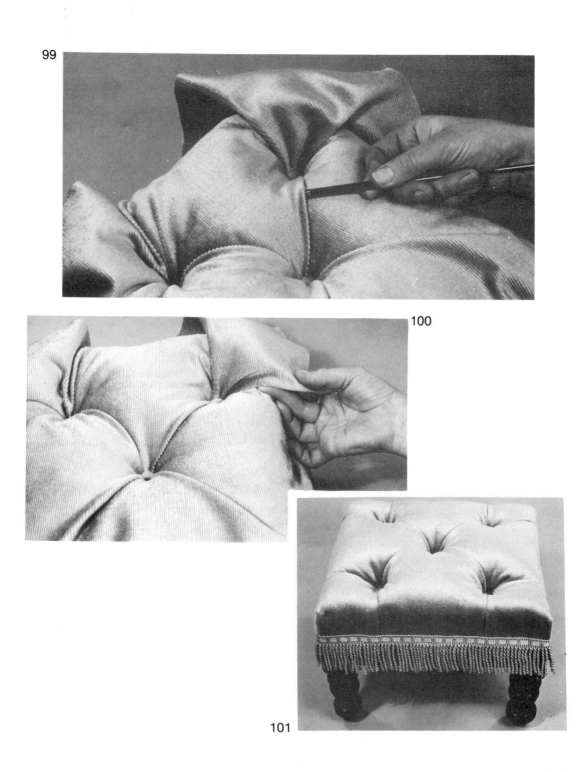

99

100

101

Child's Chair with Sewn Back

The chair shown in figure 102 is a much more ambitious project than anything tackled so far.

Preparation

Remove the existing upholstery stage by stage, laying each aside for reference. Make a note of the spring arrangement and quantity and distribution of the webbing.

    The chair consists ot a wooden seat frame that is sprung and padded in a manner similar to that described in chapter 4. This part of the work is fairly straight forward. Onto this is fixed a frame of metal struts which is padded to form the back. Being metal this precludes the use of tacks and each stage has to be sewn.

    The seat frame will have a bevelled edge to the front rail and is dealt with first.

    Figure 103 shows the cleared frame ready for work to commence.

102. Original Condition

Webbing, Springs and Stuffing

Turn the chair upside down and stretch webbing in place over the base. Remember that the springs must be adequately supported as described in chapter 4, reference to the original arrangement may well be helpful. First put in the pieces from back to front, then weave through those from side to side.

    Check that the springs are sound and free from distortion. Replace if necessary.

    Turn the chair the right way up and using the method described in detail in chapter 4, sew in the springs with No. 2 twine, fixing each one to the webbing at four points around its base.

103. Cleared frame

102

103

Cut suitable lengths of laid cord, (allow plenty of margin) put in temporary tacks along each rail in line with the springs and lash the springs securely to the frame. Hammer the tacks home.

Stretch a piece of 14oz. hessian across the top of the seat, turn in a hem all round and tack down with half inch tacks.

Sew the springs to the hessian with twine making three stitches around the top of each.

104. Edge roll complete

Put in bridle ties across the top of the hessian and pick in a good thick layer of horse hair across the whole seat area. The front edge and corners should be really firm to take the sewing at a later stage but around the curve of the back the stuffing should taper down to meet the fame.

When you are satisfied, cut a piece of scrim 3″ larger all round than the seat frame and stretch it in place over the stuffing. At the back , just secure at three or four points along the top of the rail for the time being.

Front Edge Roll

Turn under the excess scrim along the front rail and tack down to the bevelled edge, checking that the padding is full and firm. Work around the front corners and back along the side rails as far as the first metal uprights. Finish off the edge roll at this point tacking it neatly down to the rail and cutting into the scrim to accomodate the metal upright.

Put in a row of blind stitches along the length of the roll ¼″ above the tack line. Add a row of top stitches to form a good shape to the edge and corners. The roll formed should be about the thickness of your finger.

Now work around the back of the seat turning the excess scrim under, pulling it tight and tacking it down to the top of the back rail.

Figure 104 shows this stage complete.

Stuffing Ties, Secondary Stuffing and Calico

Stab through stuffing ties around the centre area of the seat being careful to avoid the springs and the webbing underneath.

Put in bridle ties across the top of the scrim and build up a layer of horse hair to fill out the shape of the seat but tapering away to nothing around the curve of the back rail.

Cut a piece of calico 3″ larger all round than the top of the seat, lay it in place and fix with temporary ⅜″ tacks along the front rail. Stretch it over the stuffing and pull it down over the back rail, cutting into the edge of the material to accomodate the uprights of the back.

Work around the sides in a similar manner, adjusting irregularities in the stuffing and adding a little wadding where the edge roll finishes to pad out any unevenness. Tack down and trim off excess. See figure 105.

Leave the seat at this stage until the padding of the back is complete.

105. Seat in calico

The Back

Cut a piece of 14 oz. hessian 2″ larger all round than the back of the frame. The simplest way is to first make a template of brown paper and use this as a pattern. Lay the template on the hessian with the bottom edge in line with the weave of the material and cut round it leaving the margin required.

Fit the hessian around the back of the frame, turning the border over in front and pinning it temporarily in place until you are sure it is right. (See figure 106). When you are satisfied, take a half round needle and sew the hessian in place with No. 2 twine. Use a simple running stitch as shown. Sew along the bottom first, then around the top, pulling the hessian tight over the back of the frame as you go.

106. Fitting and stitching the hessian

Preparing the Edge Roll

Mark in on the hessian the centre point of the top of the back with a felt tip pen, then mark off all round the top rail at 6″ intervals. Measure and mark off a 2″ border all round inside the top of the back.

Cut a strip of scrim long enough to go around the top edge of the frame plus 6″ over at each end, with one long edge being a selvedge edge. (This prevents fraying). In the example shown the strip was cut 7″ wide, for a full size chair 12–13″ should be sufficient.

Mark in the centre point on each long edge of the strip of scrim, then mark off the selvedge edge at 6″ intervals to each end.

Offer up the centre mark on the selvedge edge of the scrim to the centre point of the border on the back and pin in place. See figure 107. Now work around the chair pinning each scrim mark to the border directly opposite the appropriate mark on the back. Where the back curves down you will find the scrim is quite loose and baggy, on the straight sections quite tight (see figure 107). Where the back curves out again to form the arms, you will find the marks will no longer line up. Just pin the scrim to the border without leaving any slack.

Using a half round needle and No. 2 twine, stitch the edge of the scrim to the hessian with a simple running stitch. Around the top corners where the scrim is slack make pleats to take up the spare material. See figure 108. Work from the centre round to the base of each arm.

Now lift the free edge of the scrim up and pin it at three or four inch intervals to the top edge of the chair back, thus forming as it were a pocket around the top edge of the back.

107. *Pinning on the scrim border*

108. *Sewing on the scrim*

109. *The form of the edge roll*

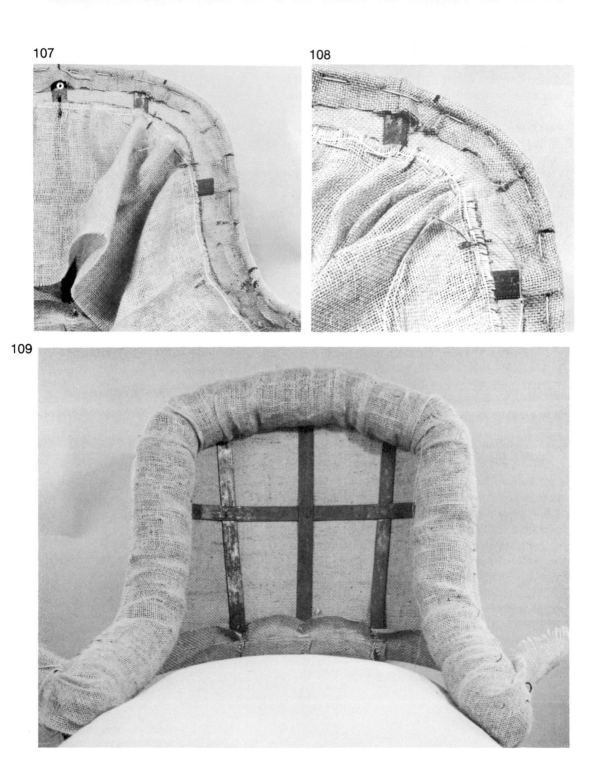

107

108

109

Padding-out the Edge Roll

Starting at the centre of the back, release the pins two or three at a time and pad out the border with fibre as shown in figure 109. As you complete each section of the stuffing the top edge of the hessian is tucked under and sewn in place along the top of the back. To do this, thread a half round needle with fine twine, take a small stitch in the centre of the top edge of the back through the hessian and then just catching the scrim into place and tie a knot.

Take another similar stitch 1" to the left through the top edge of the hessian and then through the scrim just catching it into place. Now slip the needle up under the twine loop between the stitches and through the stitch itself to form a knot. See figure 110. Pull tight and continue around the frame in each direction.

At this stage the roll formed must be full and firmly rounded or there will not be enough play in the hessian for the next stage.

Sewing the Roll

Thread a half round needle with No. 2 twine and secure in the centre of the top of the back as before. Insert the regulator needle into the front of the roll and lift the fibre up and back so that the body of the roll is drawn onto the top of the back to form a pad along the metal frame.

Pass the half round needle right through the roll 1½" to the left and then back again ¾" to the right. Slip the needle through the stitch to form a knot and pull tight. Figures 111 and 112 show diagramatically and practically what is required.

110. Top edge of scrim being sewn to the frame

111. Section through roll before and after stitching

112. Stitching the roll

104

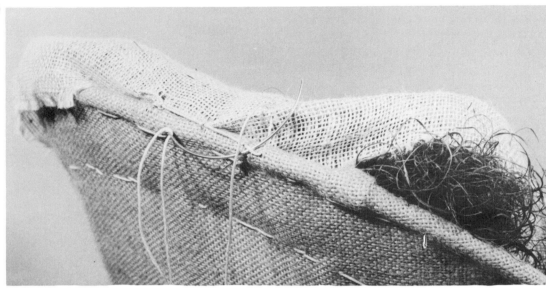

110

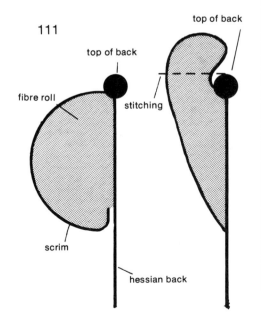

111

top of back

fibre roll

scrim

top of back

stitching

hessian back

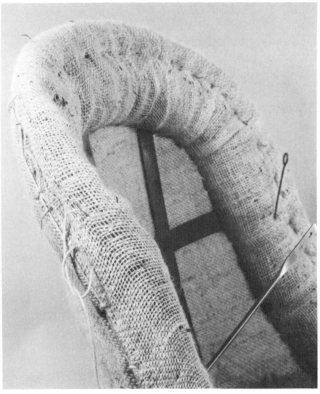

112

Work right round the top edge of the frame in each direction bringing enough fibre up with the regulator to make a firm pad above the line of the stitching. At the ends of the arms cut off any excess scrim and finish neatly.

Padding-out the Back

The first step is to complete the edge roll around the inside bottom rail of the back as shown in figure 113. Cut a piece of scrim a little longer than the gap to be filled and about 12″ deep. Sew one edge of this to the bottom inside edge of the back, then lift up and pack with fibre as before. Tuck in the top edge of the scrim and sew tightly back to the hessian as shown, using the regulator needle to adjust the fibre to a good shape.

Put bridle ties over the whole area of the back and pick in a good thick layer of horse hair. Make it very deep in the centre area, gradually tapering off towards the edges to allow for the depth of the roll underneath.

113.   Edge roll complete

Calico

114.   Calico cover

Cut a piece of calico the shape of the back plus a 6″ margin all round. Cut off the arm sections which must be fitted seperately and lay it in place over the stuffing. Tuck the bottom edge back underneath the stuffing until you can reach it from the back of the chair. Pin it carefully around the bottom edge of the back and then sew it in place with twine. Attach the two arm pieces in the same manner so that they overlap about an inch each side.

Pull the calico tightly up over the back and top rail and pin down to the hessian of the back. Add more hair where required to give a good shape over the top of the frame and then sew the calico in place as shown in figure 114.

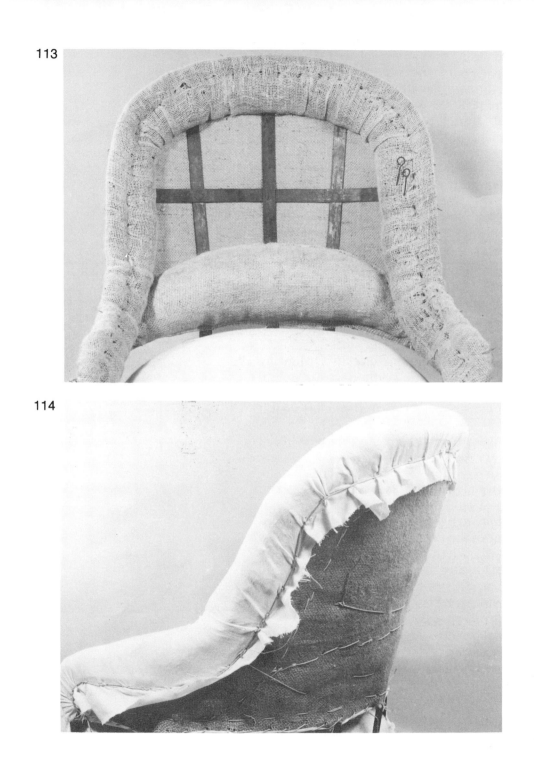

113

114

Start from the centre and sew round in each direction using the same stitch as when sewing the edge roll. 1½" forward, ¾" back, slip the needle through the stitch to form a knot and pull tight. Gather the fullness of the material into the knotted portion of the stitch.

Shaping the Back

Sew in a row of stitches tightly across the back to form the shaping. Use a double bayonet needle and stab right through the back as shown in figure 115.

The Cover

The seat cover must be put on first.

Cut a piece of skin wadding to cover the seat and lay it in place skin side up. Trim it to fit neatly around the front and sides.

Cut a piece of cover material to size leaving a 3" margin all round. If you have not got an old cover to use as a pattern, cut a paper pattern first to make sure that you have got it right.

Lay the cover in place and fix with three temporary tacks underneath the front rail. Now work around the back and sides pulling the material through and cutting into it to allow it to pass between the metal back supports. Fix each section with temporary tacks. Remember the front section at each side must be tacked underneath the rail. When you are satisfied, return to complete the front rail, turning in the corners with a single pleat as shown in figure 116. Hammer home the tacks and trim off excess material.

Next comes the front of the back.

Cut a piece of skin wadding to cover the back and lay it in place. Mould it to the shape of the upholstery, cutting into it to trim away excess fullness where required.

115.   Shaping

116.   The seat cover

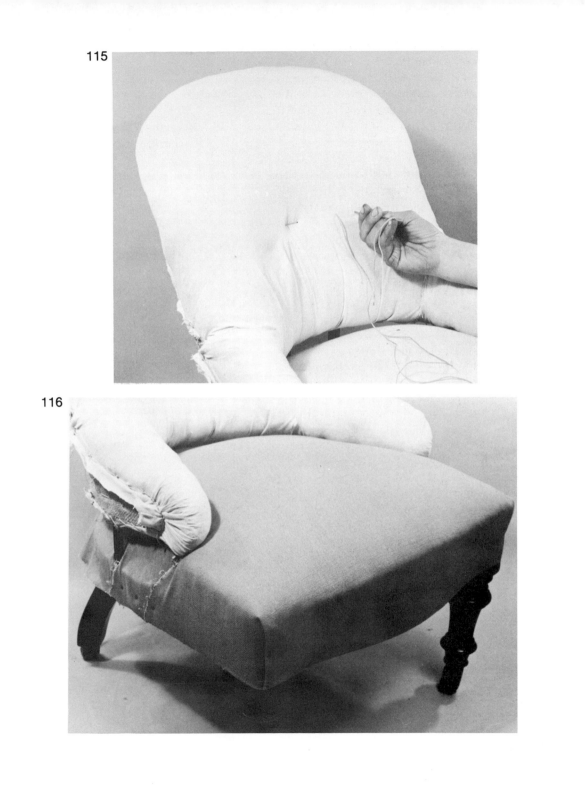

115

116

Cut a piece of cover material large enough to cover the back excluding the arm sections, plus a 6″ margin at the top and bottom. Where the shaping comes sew a folded piece of spare material onto the back of the cover as shown in figure 117. Now secure 4 or 6 short lengths of twine into the scrap as shown.

With the double bayonet needle, thread each length of twine and stab through to the back of the chair. Tie alternate twine ends together to hold the shaping in place.

Draw the bottom edge of the cover down through the seat, cutting into the material to allow it to pass between the back supports and temporarily tack each section to the seat frame. Stretch and sew the top edge of the cover as for the calico.

Now cut the arm sections and slip stitch them on to the main body of the cover using the method described when finishing the padded box. You will need to release some of the temporary tacks holding the base of the cover while you do this. Tack the arm sections to the seat frame at the base and sew at the top as before. See figure 118. Hammer home the tacks.

Finally cut the back of the cover to include the arms leaving a 3″ margin all round and starting at the top centre of the back rail turn under a hem and slip stitch it into place as shown.

Cover the base with black upholstery linen. Figure 119 shows the chair complete

117. Twine anchors for shaping sewn in

118. Sewing on the cover

119. Chair complete

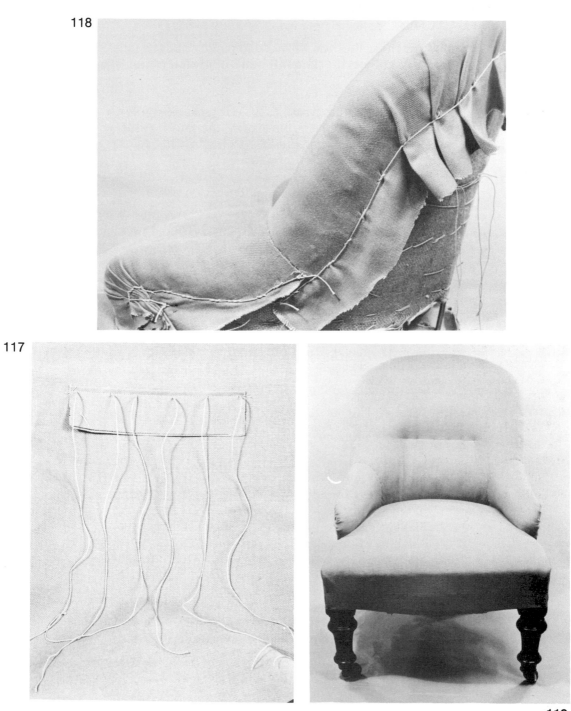

118

117

119

Basic Tools

The tools listed below are those that you will need to make a start. If you enjoy the craft there will be others that you will want to buy later, that is part of the fun of it.

Ripping Chisel: Used in clearing the frame to lift old tacks or staples. Comes in straight or cranked form, the latter, (illustrated), is probably most useful to begin with.

Mallet: For use with ripping chisel above.

Hammer: Illustrated is a good basic model to start with. A hammer with a small head would also be useful.

Shears: Heavier than dressmakers' shears, are available in different sizes. 9″ or 10″ are adequate for most jobs.

Scissors: A pair with good sharp points.

Knife: Must be kept sharp.

Webbing Stretcher: A number of different types are available. That illustrated works well and is probably the most common.

File or Rasp: For forming the bevelled edge.

Pincers: Useful for removing headless tacks.

Tape Measure: A dressmakers tape measure is ideal.

Skewers: Used in some types of work for holding stuffing, etc. temporarily in place.

Tailors' Chalk: For marking measurements, etc, on back of fabric.

Needles:
1. Regulator – for adjusting stuffing and for forming pleats in fabric.
2. Half-round – for putting in bridle ties and general stitching.
3. Springing – for sewing springs to webbing and hessian.
4. Slipping – for stitching sections of the cover together where tacks cannot be used.
5. Double Bayonet – a versatile needle with two points used in many stitching operations. Can also be used for buttoning.
6. Straight, Buttoning – a fine, straight needle for buttoning.

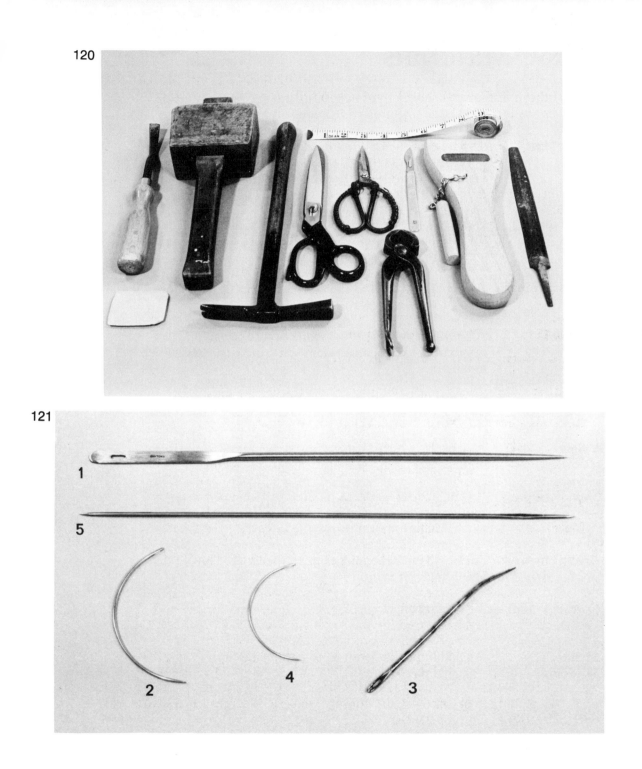

Basic Materials

In any craft it is a false economy to use anything but the best materials. Listed below is a good basic selection which you will need to start with.

Horse Hair   The traditional material used for stuffing. Difficult to obtain new and second-hand needs cleaning and teasing out. A well worth while but messy task. Hair mixtures are available but expensive.

Coir Fibre: Ginger fibre or coconut fibre used for initial stages of the padding in some seats. A relatively soft fibre that will compress a lot.

Algerian Fibre: A more robust fibre than coir. Suitable for use where greater resilience is required.

Hessian: A coarse, woven material made of jute. Available in a number of widths and weights. 12 oz. is suitable for most work.

Scrim: Similar to hessian but a more open weave and made of flax.

Calico: A closely woven cotton material usually used in unbleached form, available in various widths.

Skin Wadding: A thin layer of wadding bonded to a skin of cotton or synthetic fabric used to prevent hairs from the stuffing working their way through the cover.

Black Linen: For lining back the underside of the work. These days often made of cotton.

Cotton Wadding: A soft cotton wool like substance used for the top layer of padding.

Synthetic Wadding: Available in sheets of various thicknesses.

114

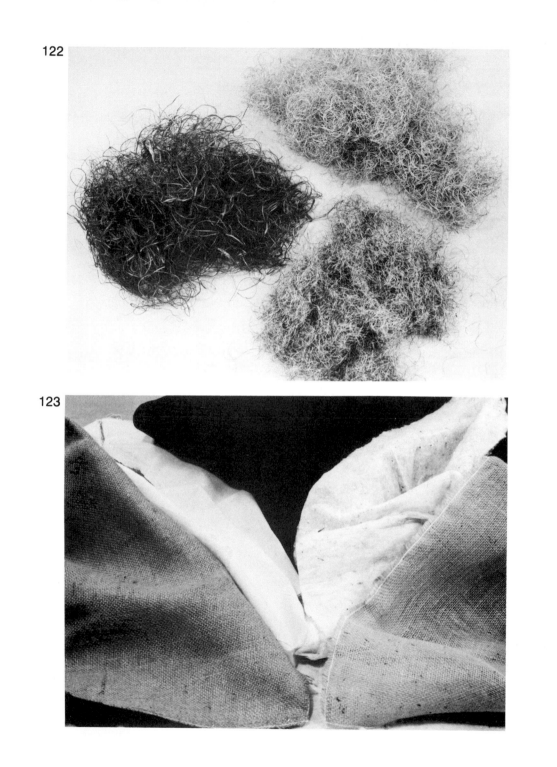

122

123

Webbing: Available in two grades, the best being black and white in colour. 2″ or 2½″ in width.

Twine: In general use 3 sizes are available. No. 2 is a good middle of the road thickness to begin with.

Laid Cord: A thick cord made of hemp used for lashing the springs to the frame.

Springs: Double cone springs made of steel, available in a range of sizes and gauges.

Tacks: The sizes most used are ⅜″, ½″ and ⅝″. In 'fine' or 'improved' qualities, the latter being the heavier gauge.

Gimp Pins: Small pins for fixing gimp or braid available in a range of colours.

Back-tacking Strip: Composition strip about ½″ in width used in back tacking. A strip of thick card will work as well.

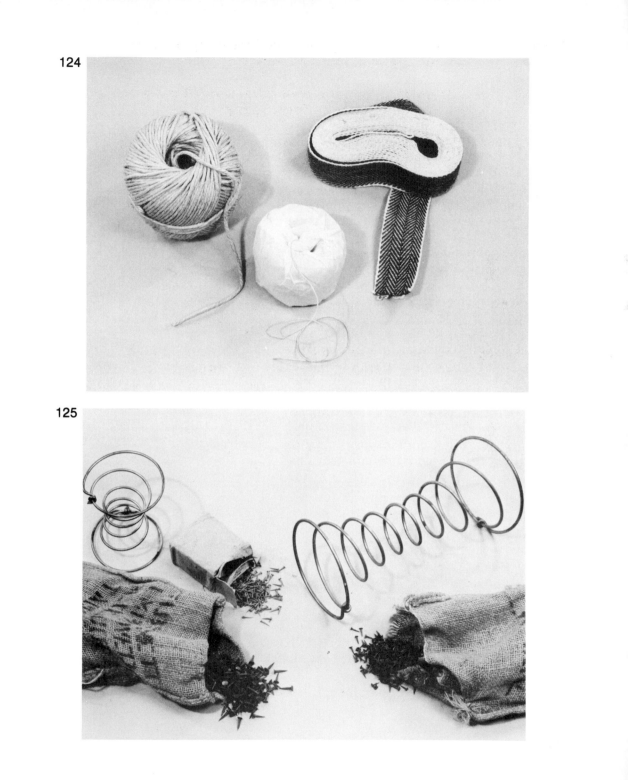

124

125

Use of Tools

Of the tools used in upholstery work, the two that are most likely to be unfamiliar to beginners are the ripping chisel and the webbing stretcher.

The ripping chisel is used in the preparatory stages of work to remove the tacks that hold the old upholstery to the frame. Place the blade edge of the chisel against the head of the tack and tap the handle with a mallet so that the blade is forced underneath the tack head. Then tip the chisel back toward the seat and prise the tack free. In practise you will find that this sequence becomes one simple movement.

Always work in the direction of the grain, ie. along the rail, to minimise the possibility of damage to the wood. See figure 126.

Figures 127 and 128 show the webbing stretcher in operation. A loop of the webbing in threaded through the slit in the stretcher and secured by the wooden pin. The stretcher is then tipped away from the work, trapping the webbing against the frame and providing the tension required.

126. Ripping chisel in use

127. Threading the stretcher

128. Tensioning the webbing

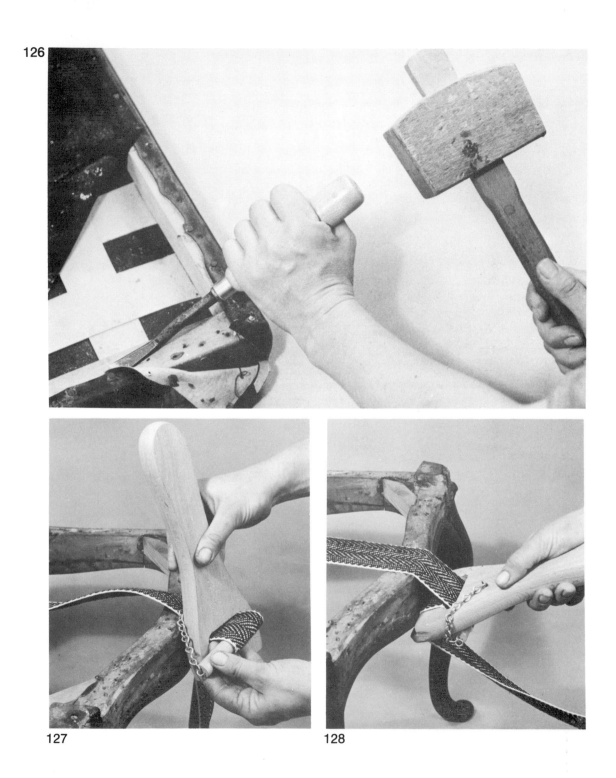

126

127

128

Anne Morrow
LINDBERGH

Anne Morrow at age 22

Anne Morrow
LINDBERGH
Pilot and Poet

Roxane Chadwick

Lerner Publications Company ▪ Minneapolis

This book is available in two editions:
Library binding by Lerner Publications Company
Soft cover by First Avenue Editions
241 First Avenue North
Minneapolis, Minnesota 55401

To Chris

LIBRARY OF CONGRESS CATALOGING-IN-PUBLICATION DATA

Chadwick, Roxane.
  Anne Morrow Lindbergh : pilot and poet.

  (The Achievers)
  Summary: A biography of the poet, essayist, and pilot
who flew with her husband, Charles A. Lindbergh around
the world charting new routes for airlines.
  1. Lindbergh, Anne Morrow, 1906–   –Biography–
Juvenile literature. 2. Authors, American–20th century–
Biography–Juvenile literature. 3. Air pilots–United
States–Biography–Juvenile literature. [1. Lindbergh,
Anne Morrow, 1906–   . 2. Authors, American. 3. Air pilots]
I. Title. II. Series.
PS3523.I516Z6 1987   818'.5209 [B] [92]   87-4242
ISBN 0-8225-0488-X (lib. bdg.)
ISBN 0-8225-9516-8 (pbk.)

Manufactured in the United States of America

International Standard Book Number: 0-8225-0488-X (lib. bdg.)
International Standard Book Number: 0-8225-9516-8 (pbk.)
Library of Congress Catalog Card Number: 82-4242

1 2 3 4 5 6 7 8 9 10 96 95 94 93 92 91 90 89 88 87

ANNE MORROW LINDBERGH: PILOT AND POET

Ten-year-old Anne Morrow looked out her bedroom window at the trees and roofs of the waking town of Englewood, New Jersey. The small brunette with large blue eyes dreamily rested her chin on the windowsill. She had recently started to keep a diary of her thoughts, and the window seat had become her favorite writing spot. From her window, she saw two big oak trees that stood beyond her family's acre of garden. She called those two trees "the married ones" and wrote about them in her new diary. Anne hoped that someday she would be able to write something honest, moving, and beautiful.

The aroma of toast called Anne downstairs, where her mother was preparing breakfast. The other Morrow children were already at the table: Elisabeth, who was 12; Dwight, 8; and Constance, 3.

Down the steps after Anne came her father, Dwight Morrow, Sr., boldly whistling a tune and unaware that the melody was all mixed-up. When he appeared, the children all rushed to kiss him, almost knocking the small man over.

This particular morning, breakfast became an ordeal for Anne when Mr. Morrow began drilling his children on their multiplication tables. He enjoyed this game, but Anne did not. "Anne, what's eight times five?" he asked. As usual, Anne drew a blank at her father's rapid question, looking down at her lap with her last bite of eggs stuck in her throat. She knew the answer was 40, but she was too shy to speak. Mr. Morrow thought these breakfast quizzes were educational, even for his quiet daughter.

Mr. Morrow and his wife, Elizabeth Cutter Morrow, felt that education was the most important thing parents could give to their children. To increase her children's knowledge, Mrs. Morrow read the children's classics to them and exposed them to fine music and art. Elizabeth Cutter Morrow combined the roles of wife and mother with a career as a writer, a teacher, and a leader in national organizations. She wrote poetry and children's books and also encouraged her children to write stories, plays, and poems.

Anne's father, Dwight Whitney Morrow

Anne's father felt the reason for his own success was his desire for knowledge. He had been a poor boy who was blessed with extraordinary intellect, energy, and charm. He had worked his way through Amherst College and Columbia Law School by tutoring other students. After law school, he had become a corporate lawyer.

In 1916, when Anne was 10, Mr. Morrow left law and went into banking as a partner in the famous international firm of J.P. Morgan and Company. He made frequent business trips abroad and often took his family with him to such cities as London, Paris, and Geneva. Morrow thought travel was educational, and he familiarized his children with the historical highlights of Europe. Even the family's winter holidays in the Bahamas and vacations at their summer home in Maine were used for reading and learning.

When Anne was a girl, her world was her family, travel, and books. She recalls being scarcely aware of World War I, except in a superficial way. Although she heard the popular songs like "Over There," saw the recruiting posters that said, "I Want YOU," and saw photographs of the war in the newspapers, nothing changed in her sheltered daily life except when one of her parents had to be away from home. Mr. Morrow served on the Allied Maritime Shipping Council, which coordinated the shipping of soldiers, food, and supplies for the Allies. Mrs. Morrow organized the first U. S. Women's Relief Unit and traveled to France to investigate its work there.

When Anne was 14, she attended Miss Chapin's School for Girls in New York City, where her family had an apartment. Instead of spending time with her schoolmates, Anne chose to write, and she preferred staying at home with her family to participating in sports and attending parties. Many years later, in the introduction to her letters and diaries, Anne would call herself the shiest, most self-conscious adolescent who ever lived.

Although Anne was timid, she was strong willed and hard working. She also had big dreams and hopes. One of the school's traditions was to have students fill out a questionnaire about their plans after graduation. In one of her answers, Anne wrote, "I want to marry a hero." At that time, the attractive girl with her head in books seemed too fearful of social gatherings to fulfill that dream.

In the autumn of 1924, Anne, following in her mother's footsteps, entered Smith College in Northampton, Massachusetts. Mrs. Morrow had been one of Smith's early graduates. She had remained active in its administration and later would serve as the college's acting president. Anne's sister Elisabeth was a junior at Smith and an excellent student. Anne was envious of her sophisticated and beautiful older sister and marveled at Elisabeth's ability to put people at ease. While Anne's grades were not as outstanding as her sister's, she did begin to excel in writing. She majored in English and worked hard, spending long hours rewriting her essays and book reviews.

10

Elizabeth Cutter Morrow, Anne's mother

In Anne's junior year, President Calvin Coolidge appointed her father as the U.S. ambassador to Mexico. When Anne and Elisabeth took the train to join their family there during Christmas vacation in Anne's senior year, they discovered that Ambassador Morrow had also invited a celebrity to Mexico for the holidays—the young and handsome Colonel Charles A. Lindbergh. Charles Lindbergh had been the first person to fly solo across the Atlantic Ocean. Earlier that year, he had flown from New York to Paris in his silver plane, the *Spirit of St. Louis*.

Ambassador and Mrs. Morrow and their youngest daughter, Constance, with Charles Lindbergh during his 1927 visit to the Morrow home in Mexico City

On May 20, 1927, Charles Lindbergh had begun his nonstop flight from New York to Paris in the *Spirit of St. Louis*.

Anne's father hoped the visit of the popular hero would ease the tension between the United States and Mexico.

Anne was determined not to worship the tall, slim hero whom the newspapers called the "Lone Eagle." To her surprise, she found Lindbergh to be serious, intelligent, optimistic—and very charming. Anne's shyness kept her from talking with Charles Lindbergh very much, but she paid a lot of attention to his mother, Evangeline Lindbergh, during her stay at the embassy in Mexico City. Her older sister, however, talked easily with the aviator, and Anne found herself envious of Elisabeth's friendliness.

13

Anne Morrow

At the time, Anne Morrow was 21, a tiny brunette who appeared to be shy and fragile. Those who knew her well, however, said she had the courage of a tigress and a stubborn determination that usually got her what she wanted. She was also sensitive and intelligent. Anne, however, did not recognize her good characteristics and wrote in her diaries of her feelings of inferiority next to her sisters—the cheerful, uninhibited Constance and the regal and beautiful Elisabeth.

14

When Ambassador Morrow took his family and the 25-year-old Colonel Lindbergh sightseeing, a crowd pushed around the car yelling, "*Viva*, Lindbergh!" Anne was so frightened by the force and size of the throng that she shrank down in her seat. Though somewhat embarrassed by the hero worship, Lindbergh just smiled and waved.

To thank the Morrows for their kindness, Charles took them flying. At first, Anne was afraid to look down, but, when her curiosity finally overcame her fear, she watched the plane's shadow on the miniature world below. Anne had found a new way of looking at things and had discovered "the fundamental magic of flying."

The world of action that Lindbergh and flying represented was very different from Anne's world of books and thoughts, but it fascinated her. When the flight was over, Elisabeth mentioned that she wanted to learn to fly, and Constance and Anne said they would, too. Lindbergh was pleased and, for the first time during his stay, seemed at ease. At the end of Lindbergh's stay, Dwight Morrow invited him to visit their house in Maine the next summer.

Charles Lindbergh was different from the well-educated, literary men Anne had known. He did not spend his time reading; instead, he lived in a world of activity and technology that was foreign to her. Anne felt she had missed something in her life. From her diary entries, it was obvious that Anne was falling in love with Lindbergh but, at the same time, she was convinced he had not even noticed her.

When Anne returned to college, she tried to learn everything she could about aviation. She read flying magazines and books and spent time at a nearby airfield asking questions of the pilots. Finally, she talked a pilot into taking her for a ride in an open-cockpit biplane.

Despite her new interest in flying, Anne's college work did not suffer. To her delight, one of her poems, "Height," appeared in *Scribner's Magazine*. At her graduation in 1928, Anne was awarded two literary prizes. One was for the most original piece of literary work, and the other for the best essay about eighteenth-century women.

Although Charles Lindbergh was not able to visit the Morrows that summer, Anne received a surprise phone call from him at her family's New York apartment in October. He was delighted with Anne's interest in flying and invited her for a ride in his silver biplane. Once they were in the air, Charles let Anne take over the controls. They flew over New York City and nearby New Jersey.

Carried out mostly in airplanes, their secret courtship was kept from the press. Anne and Charles met at friends' houses, borrowed cars, and flew from open fields instead of from airports to avoid reporters. Sometimes they would escape through cellar windows or wear disguises. By December, they were secretly engaged.

Anne knew her marriage to Charles seemed somewhat of a mismatch. Charles was a man of action; Anne was a woman of thoughts. Charles was a public hero; Anne was a very private person. But Anne had three qualities she

Charles Lindbergh ready to take off on his transatlantic flight

felt necessary to make their marriage work: courage, strength, and a sense of humor.

In February, Ambassador Morrow announced the engagement of his daughter to Charles Lindbergh. Public interest was high because Anne was both personally attractive and from a prominent American family. The public now considered Anne's life their property.

When a couple becomes engaged, it is usually the man who is congratulated. But for Anne and Charles, the opposite happened. Anne was congratulated for capturing the hero of the hour. A member of the American embassy in Mexico sang a song calling her "only the ambassador's daughter" but referring to Charles as "the Prince of the air." Everyone, including Anne, thought the song was funny—but basically true.

On May 27, 1929, Anne's father invited close friends and relatives to a reception for Charles's mother at the Morrows' new estate in Englewood, Next Day Hill. When the ambassador appeared with Anne solemnly holding his arm, it became obvious there was a different reason for the gathering. Anne was wearing a white wedding dress and carrying a bouquet of spring flowers that Elisabeth had picked earlier that morning. By surprising even their guests, Anne and Charles managed to be married without the intrusion of the press.

Outside the gate to the Morrow estate, a group of reporters were waiting for Charles, as usual. When he sped past them in a car, he appeared to be alone, but his new bride was lying on the floor beside him. The newlyweds escaped undetected to a 38-foot cabin cruiser, the *Mouette*, for a honeymoon voyage from Long Island to Maine.

To give the couple a head start, the party in Englewood continued. Hours later, the press was told about the marriage. Then the hunt began. Every reporter wanted to be the first to photograph the new Mrs. Lindbergh. Two days later, the Lindberghs were spotted. A reporter and a cameraman circled the couple's boat for seven hours, requesting them to pose. Anne and Charles wanted only to be left alone and escaped temporarily by heading out to sea.

In marrying Charles, Anne had given up her protected home life and had become a partner to the international hero, sharing in both his triumphs and his trials. From the start of their marriage, Charles made it clear to Anne that his idea of a wife was not one who sat at home and waited for him. Instead, he wanted her to be a working partner.

Although Anne hated the publicity, she loved her new world. She took flying lessons from her perfectionist husband, soloing for the first time on August 29, 1929, and in 1930 became the first U.S. woman to get a glider pilot's license. Soon she earned her license in an engine-driven plane and then learned to use the radio. She became swift and accurate at using Morse code—the means of communication between air and ground in 1930—and learned to read navigational charts to pinpoint their plane's location, even when flying over the sea or in darkness.

Anne and Charles Lindbergh shortly after their marriage

As a survey team, Charles and Anne flew various routes across the United States for Transcontinental Air Transport (now Trans World Airlines) and over South America for Pan American Airways. They reported on weather and landing conditions to help the airlines find the safest routes for passenger service.

Although Anne referred to herself as Charles's faithful page, she had indeed become his working partner. As copilot and navigator, Anne did a good job. Her confidence was boosted when Charles said no woman ever existed who was her equal. The satisfaction of expanding her abilities was only part of Anne's enjoyment. She loved the beauty of flight and her new view of the world. She enjoyed the thrill of the engine's roar, the power of controlling the plane, and the excitement of seeing new places. Anne called these early years of her marriage when she was sharing flying adventures with her new husband "the golden years."

On April 20, 1930, the couple flew from Los Angeles to New York in 14 hours and 45 minutes, breaking the transcontinental speed record. They flew in a new plane, the *Sirius*, that Charles had designed for survey flying. This trip, however, was not as pleasant for Anne because she was seven months pregnant. Bad weather surrounded their air route, and, to avoid the storms, they had to fly higher than was good for Anne's health. Although painfully sick, she continued to do her tasks.

The pride of doing a good job on their flights and the

rewards of fame were dampened for the Lindberghs by the lack of privacy in their lives. Wherever the couple went, flocks of people and reporters pushed forward to talk to them. They could not shop, go to a theater, or eat at a restaurant without being mobbed. The more uncooperative Anne and Charles became, the harder the reporters tried to get an interview or take a photograph of them. The press used stories that the Lindberghs' friends or acquaintances told them. Charles warned Anne never to say, do, or write anything that she didn't want to see on the front page of a newspaper. That advice was very difficult for Anne to follow because she had always written honestly and with feeling.

When Anne and Charles were not flying, they often stayed with Anne's parents. The large Morrow estate was well protected for Mr. Morrow was now a New Jersey state senator, with aspirations to one day become president. At Next Day Hill on June 22, 1930, her 24th birthday, Anne gave birth to a son, Charles Augustus. Anne wanted to have a normal home life for her family, so the Lindberghs decided to build a house in a remote area of New Jersey.

While their new house near Hopewell was being built, Anne and Charles took off in their red-and-black monoplane to chart air routes to the Orient. The usual route to the Orient was west across the Pacific Ocean, but the Lindberghs wanted to test the possibility of using the Great Circle Route. This route, the shortest distance from New York to China, follows a straight line over Canada,

Anne with her first child, Charles Augustus, Jr.

The Lindberghs seated in a Lockheed Altair

the Arctic Sea, the U.S.S.R., Japan, and on to China.

For months, Charles planned and prepared for their adventure. The Lindberghs' plane, the *Sirius*, had two single seats, one in front of the other. It was fitted with pontoons so it could float on water, and Anne and Charles wore special flying suits that were heated by electricity to keep out the Arctic cold. The small, single-engine plane also carried emergency equipment, food rations, airplane parts, and survival gear because most of the land they would be crossing was uninhabited.

The Lindberghs were the first to fly the Great Circle Route from New York to China.

The Lindberghs began their flight to the Orient on July 27, 1931, and stopped in Aklavik, Canada (above), in August.

For the flight, Anne would be both the copilot and the radio operator. She struggled to locate radio stations to inform the world of their progress and to keep track of weather conditions ahead of them. Carefully, she tapped the dots and dashes of Morse code and then listened intently for the dot-dash-dot signal, the code for the letter *R*, which meant a station had received her message.

The Lindbergh's journey was both a difficult task and an exciting adventure. The couple endured freezing temperatures and some nights slept in their cramped plane surrounded by pea-soup fog. They survived dangerous takeoffs and terrifying landings, but they were also greeted warmly

The *Sirius* lands on a lagoon outside of Tokyo.

The Lindberghs (center) were welcomed to Japan with great enthusiasm.

by many interesting people and saw many unusual places. At a remote village on Baker Lake in the Northwest Territories of Canada, they met fur trappers, and at Barrow, the northernmost point in Alaska, some Eskimos danced for them. When they were forced down by fog into a desolate Alaskan inlet, they were surprised to find duck hunters. A group of singing sailors rescued their plane when its anchor rope broke in Japan. Just before takeoff in Osaka, Japan, the Lindberghs discovered an 18-year-old boy curled up in their plane's baggage area. He had stowed away in the *Sirius*, hoping for a ride to the United States.

28

Anne and Charles relaxing after their arrival in Japan

Finally, on September 29, 1931, Anne and Charles reached Nanking (Nanjing), China. They had proven it was possible to reach the Orient by traveling north. In China, the Lindberghs found that the great Yangtze River had flooded the countryside. Villages and crops were destroyed, and people were homeless and hungry. Charles volunteered to help the National Flood Relief Commission by mapping the damaged areas and carrying medical supplies and a doctor to the flooded areas.

A British airplane carrier, the *Hermes*, offered to keep the *Sirius* on the boat at night and out of the dangerous, turbulent currents of the river. One morning, before the seamen put the *Sirius* back into the water, Anne climbed into the back seat, and Charles got into the front seat. The *Hermes* crew lifted the aircraft by pulley and cable and carefully put the plane into the river facing the current.

Suddenly, however, something went wrong. Either the engine or the current pulled the plane out away from the ship. The crew could not release the cable, and the current was pulling one wing and one pontoon into the water. The *Sirius* and its pilots were in trouble. As Charles yelled a warning to Anne, she unbuckled her seat belt. The plane began to pivot around the wing that was under the water. The *Sirius* was tipping over.

Without hesitating, Anne stood up and jumped into the turbulant water. She went under, slipped below the plane, and popped up on the other side. Even in the swift current of the Yangtze (Chang Jiang) River, she was a good swim-

Following the accident to the *Sirius,* Anne climbs from the Yangtze (Chang Jiang) River into a rescue boat.

mer. When Charles surfaced in the murky water, he saw Anne nearby. Later he said she looked "perfectly happy paddling along like a little mud turtle." The Lindberghs were helped from the water and were safe, but the *Sirius* was badly damaged.

Shortly after the accident, Anne received a telegram from her mother telling her that her father, Dwight Morrow, Sr., had died from a cerebral hemorrhage. Anne and Charles cancelled the rest of their trip and returned home by boat.

Anne at home with her mother, Elizabeth Cutter Morrow; her grand-
mother, Annie Spencer Cutter; and her son, Charles A. Lindbergh, Jr.,
in January 1931

After two months of adventure, Anne and Charles were glad to settle down to a peaceful family life. Anne needed rest and quiet. She was tired from the trip, saddened by her father's death, and worried by her mother's deep grief. She spent much of that winter ill from off-and-on bouts of some kind of food poisoning. The persistent illness made the usually energetic and healthy Anne weak and unable to enjoy the Christmas festivities that year.

Early in February 1932, Anne, Charles, and Charles, Jr., moved into their new home. Anne was pregnant again and welcomed the privacy of their Hopewell residence. Only one road led to the house, which was surrounded by 500 acres of countryside. They had picked this homesite because the nearby swamps and mountains would keep out most intruders.

Tuesday, March 1, was cold and wet. At 6:30 in the evening, Anne and the nurse put 20-month-old Charles, Jr., in his crib on the second floor of their new home. They closed and bolted all of the shutters in the room, except one that was warped. Then they said good night to little Charles.

Around 8:30, Colonel Lindbergh returned home. At 10:00, the nurse checked on the baby and found his crib empty. On the windowsill was an envelope with a ransom note. Little Charles had been kidnapped.

Anne was numb with fear and disbelief. State troopers, photographers, and reporters overran the grounds. The Lindberghs paid the $50,000 ransom demanded, but their

The Lindbergh home near Hopewell, New Jersey

son was not returned. For 72 days, Anne lived in a whirling nightmare. The police studied the 38,000 letters and the constant telephone calls the Lindberghs received, hoping to find a clue about the kidnappers.

On May 12, Charles, Jr., was found dead near the Lindbergh's home. At that moment, Anne's interest in the case ended because she knew nothing would bring back her baby. Her happiness had been shattered, and she had to learn how to live with the memory of that cruel winter. Charles's reaction, however, was different. He worked with the police, going over every detail of the crime. But the murderer remained free.

Anne's faith in life was partially restored by the birth of another son, Jon, on August 16, 1932. When crackpot mail threatened Jon's life, the Lindberghs bought a large German shepherd named Thor to protect the baby. Then bad memories forced the Lindberghs from their home, which they donated to the state of New Jersey for use as a residence for homeless children.

Anne longed for the security of a home and the everyday tasks of caring for her new baby. While she needed a quiet life and the passing of time to ease her pain, Charles found relief in his work and busied himself planning another survey flight. Large airplanes able to carry passengers across oceans were being built, but a good route across the Atlantic was still a problem. Ironically, where the land masses were the closest, the weather was the worst.

In the summer of 1933, Anne and Charles took off to survey air routes between North America and Europe. Again, they flew the *Sirius*, which had been repaired since their accident in the Orient. They flew from New York to Greenland, where a young Eskimo boy renamed their plane the *Tingmissartoq*, meaning "the one who flies like a big bird." The Lindberghs continued their flight to Iceland, Scandinavia, the U.S.S.R., and Britain. They flew south to Spain and Africa, crossed the Atlantic Ocean again to Brazil, and then proceeded north over the Caribbean to Miami, Florida, and back to New York. The flight was an incredible aviation achievement.

Their 30,000-mile trip, however, was riddled with hazards. When the couple landed in a harbor on the east coast of Greenland, they had to guide the plane between icebergs. They braved the arctic cold, blizzards, sandstorms, hurricanes, and tropical heat. They were forced down by fog on the Minho River in Portugal, and the end of their antennae broke off because Anne didn't have enough time to wind the entire antennae in before they hit the water.

Throughout the flight, Anne showed extraordinary skill as navigator and radio operator. On the way to the Cape Verde Islands off the west coast of Africa, Anne made her regular radio calls to report the plane's position and get weather information from a nearby island. She had a few minutes to spare, so she sent out a general radio call over her shortwave, hoping that a station on the coast of South America might pick up her signal. She was listening on the radio frequency of 24 meters when she heard station WSL at Sayville, Long Island, in New York.

Impulsively, she decided to call. "WSL—WSL—WSL from KHCAL. Answer on 24," she said, giving them the frequency. To her delight, she heard, "KHCAL—KHCAL—KHCAL from WSL." The station in New York sent the Morse code signals for "QRK," which meant her message was coming through strong. Anne then received the dots and dashes for "QRU." This meant, "Do you have a message?" Anne was extremely excited because she had sent out and received messages from over more than 3,000 miles away. She tapped out the letters to say, "Lindbergh

The Lindberghs' North Atlantic survey flight covered 30,000 miles and lasted from early in July through mid-December 1933.

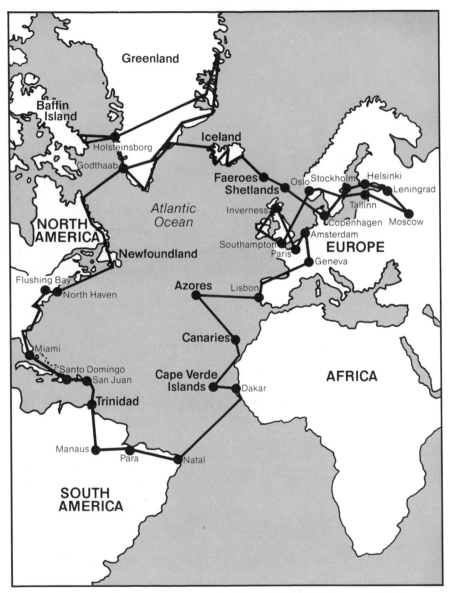

The route of the Lindberghs' North Atlantic survey flight

plane en route to Cape Verde Islands." For Anne, making that contact was the highlight of the trip.

On their flight, the Lindberghs mixed their work with pleasure. They spent a week in Cartwright, a coastal village in Canada, and a week sightseeing in the U.S.S.R. In Wales, they visited Anne's sister, Elisabeth. Ten months earlier, Elisabeth had married a Welshman named Aubrey Morgan. Since her marriage, she had suffered a heart attack, and her health had deteriorated.

During the survey flight around the North Atlantic, Anne and Charles worked together to survive. Although Anne was often frightened, the trip gave her a sense of freedom and time for some privacy with her husband. Their work, their closeness, and the passing of time began to heal their hurt over the death of Charles, Jr. But Anne was separated from the most nourishing and healing element in her life—her son, Jon.

The Lindberghs returned home just before Christmas 1933. Their dangerous flight had covered four continents and had lasted five and one-half months. They had provided Pan American Airways with enough information to establish regular passenger service between the United States and Europe within five years.

Anne's achievement as copilot and radio operator for the survey was very significant. In 1934, the National Geographic Society awarded her the Hubbard Gold Medal for distinction in exploration, research, and discovery. She was the first woman to receive the medal.

During their Atlantic trip, the Lindberghs had spent a week in the
USSR. Here Anne is greeted by a Soviet official soon after arriving
in Leningrad.

About one year after Anne and Charles returned home from the survey, Bruno Hauptmann was tried for the murder of Charles, Jr. The trial began on January 2, 1935, in Flemington, New Jersey, and lasted for six weeks. Colonel Lindbergh studied the evidence and was convinced that the murderer had been found.

Anne went to the trial only twice. The first time, when she testified, she stared out a window at a triangle of blue sky. The second time was when her mother testified. That was a terribly emotional event for Anne, and she never attended the trial again. Instead, she spent her time with her son, Jon, and tried to forget the past. When the jury condemned Hauptmann to death without mercy, Anne was glad the trial was over. She wanted to start their lives again and to build a secure and happy life for herself, Charles, and Jon.

For Anne, the year 1935 was an uphill climb out of sorrow and grief. The Lindberghs were living with Anne's mother at the Morrow estate, Next Day Hill, and Anne resented having no home of their own and no privacy. She cried silently at night or sitting on a stump in the woods outside of the fenced grounds of her mother's home. She lost the confidence she had possessed in her early years of marriage.

Amid the glare of the trial publicity, the Lindberghs took one step toward starting a normal life again when they began looking for a home of their own. Although she knew her fear was not good for him, Anne could not help worrying about Jon's safety. When he was three and one-half, Anne let him attend a nursery school called the Little School in Englewood. This was a special school to Anne because it had been established by her sister Elisabeth, who had died of pneumonia in 1934.

As Jon's nurse was driving him to school one morning, a fast car passed them, swerved, and forced them to the curb. Men poured out of the car, rushed to their vehicle, and poked huge cameras at the frightened child. When photographs of Jon crying appeared in the next morning's paper, Anne withdrew him from the school.

The Lindberghs could take no more publicity, prying, or pain. Three days before Christmas 1935, they fled from the United States aboard a passenger ship to live in England. There the Lindberghs rented an old rambling house called Long Barn. The crooked little house with tipsy floors and slanted walls was nestled against the side of a hill, and the terraced garden bloomed with flowers. Here Anne found peace and privacy. Reporters no longer hounded the family, people didn't stare, and no one bothered Jon. The family gardened in the English soil and gained strength. On May 12, 1937, Anne had another son, Land.

Besides renewing her career as a mother, Anne now had time for writing. She wanted to write so she could overcome her nagging doubts about developing an identity of her own. She had spent so much time and energy being Charles' partner that she needed some time to be herself.

Anne, Jon, and Charles Lindbergh landed in Liverpool, England, on December 31, 1935.

Between adventures over the previous four years, Anne had written her first book, *North to the Orient*. It was a very human retelling of the Lindberghs' flight to China. Rather than a factual account of the survey, it was Anne's vivid impressions of the trip. In England, Anne finished *Listen! the Wind*, a book about 10 days of the Atlantic survey flight. Like her first, this book was highly praised both as a small work of art and a valuable account of aviation history.

The years in England ended in June 1938 when the Lindberghs moved to a barren French island named Illiec. Anne had become disillusioned with England because her book was not selling well there, and she had made no friends. The final annoyance came when she flunked her English driving test, even though she had driven in the United States for 15 years without having an accident. So Anne was happy to move to the island, which was near one owned by Dr. Alexis Carrel, a Nobel Prize-winning scientist who had worked with Charles Lindbergh to invent a mechanical glass heart.

From Illiec, Anne and Charles made three trips for the United States to find out about Germany's air power. Charles found the Nazi air force impressive, and he frankly said so. He believed the German air force was larger than all the rest of Europe's forces combined, and that the United States was the only country that could stop the Germans in the air. During one of these visits in 1938, Charles accepted a medal and met several Nazi generals.

Because she felt that war was the worst evil possible, Anne shared the hope of Europeans for peace and believed that negotiations and appeasement of Adolf Hitler would prevent a war. But as the cruelty of the Nazi actions was revealed, Anne realized there were evils worse than war. In Europe, the threat of war kept increasing, and German troops were sent into Czechoslovakia and Poland. In April 1939, the Lindberghs moved back to the United States.

Anne, Charles, Jon, and Land had no home so, once again, they moved in with Anne's mother. Charles tried to persuade the United States to stay out of the war in Europe and became a spokesman for the American First Committee, an anti-war group. He criticized President Roosevelt's foreign policy, saying the president was leading the United States into an undeclared war. Anne joined the movement against war by writing a book titled *The Wave of the Future: A Confession of Faith*. The slim volume suggested the United States needed reform at home rather than a crusade abroad. The book became a best-seller, but Anne's confidence in her writing was shaken because it was criticized severely by reviewers.

Now the press began to attack the Lindberghs for their trips to Germany, and they criticized Charles for accepting the German medal and for speaking against the war. TWA removed Lindbergh's name from their airline slogan, and President Roosevelt called Charles a traitor. Angered, Charles resigned from the Army Air Corps. In a small, upstate New York town, even Anne's book *Listen! the*

Wind was banned. Ten years earlier, Anne had shared in the public's adoration of her husband. Now she shared its criticism.

During all of this turmoil, Anne gave birth to a daughter, Anne Spencer, in October of 1940. During the war years, she devoted most of her time and energy to her growing family.

When the Japanese attacked the American base of Pearl Harbor in Hawaii on December 7, 1941, the United States entered World War II. Charles tried to enlist in the Air Corps, but he was refused. Instead, he joined the war effort as a civilian, testing bombers for Henry Ford in Detroit, Michigan. There in the autumn of 1942, Anne gave birth to another child, Scott Morrow.

While Charles tested bombers, Anne raised their children and wrote. She completed *The Steep Ascent*, a fictional story about a real incident. In the book, a woman comes close to death while crossing the Alps by plane.

Anne worried when Charles was sent to the combat area as a civilian technician because she knew he was too adventurous to stay out of the action. Although a civilian, at age 42 he flew 50 combat missions, winning the respect of the younger pilots.

When the war ended, Charles returned home. The Lindberghs bought a house close to Scott's Cove near Darien, Connecticut. There they had their last child, a daughter named Reeve, in the summer of 1945. In Darien, the Lindberghs lived a quiet life out of the public eye.

Together Anne and Charles tried to teach self-reliance to their five children, who now ranged in age from 1 to 13. In the summer, the family hiked, bicycled, swam, and went on picnics. In the winter, they skied, sledded, read around the fire, and listened to music.

Anne was submerged in marketing, meal planning, the PTA, sewing, laundry, and driving children to basketball practice or orchestra rehearsal. Yet she still found time for her writing. With five active children in the house, she often escaped to a small gray toolshed that had been converted to a writing retreat. She and Charles had found the shed beside a highway many years earlier and had moved it to their backyard at Scott's Cove.

During the 1950s and 1960s, Anne wrote many kinds of books. *Gift from the Sea* was a group of essays on love, marriage, youth, and old age, all inspired by seashells. It spoke elegantly to women about a need to escape from the routines of life and seek self-fulfillment. It told what Anne had learned during her lifetime in her search for independence—that basically everyone is alone. This slim volume became a best-seller, and Anne's confidence in her writing ability was renewed.

Next, Anne finished a collection of poems, *The Unicorn and Other Poems*. After that, she wrote a novel about marriage called *Dearly Beloved: A Theme and Variations*. Her next book, *Earth Shine*, included two beautiful essays on conservation. The first told of the 1968 Apollo 8 moon shot, and the other was about a safari trip to Kenya and

Tanzania in East Africa. Then Anne compiled her letters and diaries from 1922 to 1939, which were published in four volumes. Those diaries and letters showed the pluck of a young woman meeting the challenge of life. In her books, Anne wrote honestly about the glow of adventure, the peace of family life, the burden of tragedy, and the trials of self-doubt. They fulfilled Anne's wish as a 10 year old: to be able to write something honest, moving, and beautiful.

While Anne was busy writing, Charles was still occupied with aviation. He won the Pulitzer Prize for biography for his book *The Spirit of St. Louis*, which told about his solo flight across the Atlantic. Charles was now a brigadier general in the U.S. Air Force Reserve, and he continued to advise Pan American Airways.

Anne and Charles had not only watched aviation grow, they had actively helped it to progress. When they surveyed air routes, they never thought that 30 years later men would walk on the moon. They were thrilled by the huge scientific achievements in flight.

By the late 1960s, however, the Lindberghs were wondering if science was moving ahead too fast, and they feared that progress was destroying the earth. Once again, they fought for a cause in which they both believed—this time it was conservation. Anne usually declined invitations to speak to groups, but she was troubled about the dying environment. In February 1970, she made a rare public speech at a meeting about environmental pollution

On July 20, 1969, Neil A. Armstrong and Edwin E. Aldrin, Jr., (above) became the first people to walk on the moon.

at her alma mater, Smith College. Before the group stood a small 63-year-old woman wearing a purple dress—her favorite color—her skin bronzed by the sun and the wind. As she began to speak, her soft, musical voice caught the audience's attention, and her ready smile alternated with a gentle, worried frown. As she spoke about saving the beauty of the earth, she touched her audience with honest words, clear ideas, and deep insights. When she finished, the group cheered. At the same meeting, she was awarded an honorary Doctor of Letters degree. Afterward, Anne returned to her quiet, private life.

In 1939, Anne Morrow Lindbergh had received an honorary Doctor of Letters degree from another school, Amherst College.

Another person who made aviation history at the same time as the Lindberghs was Amelia Earhart, shown here with Anne in 1930. Earhart would later make several long-distance flight records.

By this time, the Lindbergh children had grown up and left home. Anne and Charles built a smaller white cottage for themselves on their land at Scott's Cove and also spent time at their homes in Switzerland and in a deserted part of Maui, Hawaii. Despite their wealth, they lived simply.

When the doctors told Charles he was dying, he asked to be flown to Maui, his favorite place. Anne, of course, went with him. Two weeks later, on August 1, 1974, Charles Lindbergh died of cancer.

With courage and understanding, Anne faced another change in her life and began the independence of widowhood. She continued to spend time visiting her five married children and enjoying her grandchildren. For nine years, she served on the board of directors for Harcourt Brace Jovanovich, Inc., a publishing company, and she continued to write, compiling a fifth volume of her diaries and letters from 1939 to 1944.

Anne Morrow Lindbergh always wrote about her life and thoughts because for Anne, an experience was not over until it was written down and shared.

Anne Morrow Lindbergh: Pilot and Poet

In 1985, at St. Paul, Minnesota, Anne Lindbergh
unveiled a statue of her husband shown as a child and
as the pilot who flew from New York to Paris in 1927.

BOOKS BY ANNE MORROW LINDBERGH

North to the Orient, 1935

Listen! the Wind, 1938

The Wave of the Future: A Confession of Faith, 1940

The Steep Ascent, 1944

Gift from the Sea, 1955

The Unicorn and Other Poems: 1935-1955, 1956

Dearly Beloved: Theme and Variations, 1962

Earth Shine, 1969

Bring Me a Unicorn: Diaries and Letters of Anne Morrow Lindbergh, 1922-1928, 1972

Hour of Gold, Hour of Lead: Diaries and Letters of Anne Morrow Lindbergh, 1929-1932, 1973

Locked Rooms and Open Doors: Diaries and Letters of Anne Morrow Lindbergh, 1933-1935, 1974

The Flower and the Nettle: Diaries and Letters of Anne Morrow Lindbergh, 1936-1939, 1976

War Within and Without: Diaries and Letters of Anne Morrow Lindbergh, 1939-1944, 1980

ACKNOWLEDGMENTS: The photographs are reproduced through the courtesy of: pp. 1 (National Air and Space Museum), 13, 17, 37 (National Air and Space Museum), Smithsonian Institution; pp. 2, 7, 11, 12, 14, 23, 28, 31, 34, National Archives; pp. 9, 29, 32, Library of Congress; pp. 20, 24, 26, 27, 40, 43, 53, AP/Wide World Photos; p. 49, National Aeronautics and Space Administration (NASA); p. 50, Smith College Archives; p. 51, Bettmann Newsphotos; p. 54, Harcourt Brace Jovanovich, Inc. (© Richard W. Brown). Front cover: National Archives (insert) and National Air and Space Museum, Smithsonian Institution. Back cover: Harcourt Brace Jovanovich, Inc. (© Richard W. Brown).

56